TIPTOE THROUGH THE TOMBSTONES

A Comedy Thriller

by Norman Robbins

samuelfrench.co.uk

THINKING ABOUT PERFORMING A SHOW?

There are thousands of plays and musicals available to perform from Samuel French right now, and applying for a licence is easier and more affordable than you might think

From classic plays to brand new musicals, from monologues to epic dramas, there are shows for everyone.

Plays and musicals are protected by copyright law so if you want to perform them, the first thing you'll need is a licence. This simple process helps support the playwright by ensuring they get paid for their work, and means that you'll have the documents you need to stage the show in public.

Not all our shows are available to perform all the time, so it's important to check and apply for a licence before you start rehearsals or commit to doing the show.

LEARN MORE & FIND THOUSANDS OF SHOWS

Browse our full range of plays and musicals and find out more about how to license a show

www.samuelfrench.co.uk/perform

Talk to the friendly experts in our Licensing team for advice on choosing a show, and help with licensing

plays@samuelfrench.co.uk   020 7387 9373

Acting Editions

BORN TO PERFORM

Playscripts designed from the ground up to work the way you do in rehearsal, performance and study

---

Larger, clearer text for easier reading

Wider margins for notes

Performance features such as character and props lists, sound and lighting cues, and more

---

+ CHOOSE A SIZE AND STYLE TO SUIT YOU

  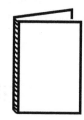

STANDARD EDITION

Our regular paperback book at our regular size

SPIRAL-BOUND EDITION

The same size as the Standard Edition, but with a sturdy, easy-to-fold, easy-to-hold spiral-bound spine

LARGE EDITION

A4 size and spiral bound, with larger text and a blank page for notes opposite every page of text. Perfect for technical and directing use

LEARN MORE | **samuelfrench.co.uk/actingeditions**

Other plays by NORMAN ROBBINS
published and licensed by Samuel French

Full-length plays:

A Tomb with a View
(*the first of the* Tomb Trilogy)

And Evermore Shall Be So

At the Sign of the "Crippled Harlequin"

The Borzoletti Monstrance

The Late Mrs Early

Nightmare

Practice to Deceive

Prepare To Meet Thy Tomb
(*the third of the* Tomb Trilogy)

Prescription For Murder

Pull The Other One

Slaughterhouse

Swan Song

Wedding of the Year

Pantomimes:

Aladdin

Ali Baba and the Forty Thieves

Babes in the Wood

FIND PERFECT PLAYS TO PERFORM AT
www.samuelfrench.co.uk/perform

AUTHOR'S NOTE

Since the publication of *A Tomb with a View* in 1978, I've had constant requests from theatre groups and audiences around the world to write a sequel. Flattering as this is, I never seemed able to come up with a suitable plot...hardly surprising as most of the characters in the original were dead by the time the final curtain fell. I toyed briefly with a prequel, but finally, after a twenty year lapse, I offer this follow-up to the Tomb family saga.

Just a brief word of advice. As in *A Tomb with a View*, what the audience sees is not always what it appears to be. The character of Vernon, for instance, though outwardly a stereotype homosexual, turns out to be something completely different from the audience's original perception. The eventual reaction to his true identity should be felt throughout the auditorium. Almost all the characters, in fact, should be played on the verge of caricature, though with great sincerity, and I'd like to stress again that the play is a spoof. A gentle homage to the kind of comedy thriller that dominated the repertory scene when I was a young actor in the fifties. Hopefully, however, it will present an intriguing mystery too.

One small production point. It would be wise to engage the ASM (or someone of a similar build to the Clown) to don the costume for the "quick change" parts of the script. It saves the actor from having a heart attack during performances.

Norman Robbins

CHARACTERS

VERNON PREWITT
EDNA HONEYWILL
ZOE MAPLETON
MORTIMER CRAYLE
OCTAVIA TOMB
HENRIETTA TOMB
AUGUSTUS TOMB
ATHENE TOMB
LARRY LEWISS
FABIA TOMB

The action of the play takes place in the library of Monument House, the decaying Gothic home of the late Tomb family, some fifty miles from London.

for

Elaine McClure

Undisputed ruler of the other Marsh

ACT I

Scene One

The library of Monument House. A Friday evening in November.

The room is dominated by an immense black walnut fireplace in the centre of the rear wall. Outsize vases rest on the outer edges of the mantel. Above the mantel, a thick gold frame holds a terrifying portrait of the late Septimus Tomb; gaunt, wrinkled, almost bald, with the bloodshot eyes of a raving lunatic. The eyes appear to follow whoever is in the room. A heavily carved wooden fender protects against sparks from the log fire, and huge firedogs of brass with attendant implements are in position. A thick hearthrug is in front of the fender. Massive empty bookcases, their dusty shelves protected by fine mesh doors, are built into the walls on either side of the fireplace. The one on the left, however, conceals a secret door that opens on a pivot into the room. The wall right is dominated by great french windows. Thick velvet drapes hang from a matching pelmet, and coffee-coloured net curtains obscure a view of overgrown shrubs outside. Meshed, empty bookcases fill the wall space on either side of the windows. Below the windows, and slightly into the room, a small octagonal table is set. On it stand several cut glass decanters containing brightly coloured liquids and a collection of glasses and goblets. Beside the table is a comfortable leather wing chair on a swivel or easy glide castors. In the opposite wall are massive Gothic doors of black walnut, each door having a large brass knob. These double doors form the only obvious entrance into the room. When they are open, a glimpse of the wide hall can be seen. Up stage of the doors is an old-fashioned roll-top desk. The top is open and a collection of quill pens, inkwell, papers, etc. can be seen. Over the desk is another empty, meshed bookcase. An outdated internal telephone is fixed to the wall down stage of this. Down stage of the doors, meshed, empty bookcases fill the remaining space. Opposite the drinks table is a matching one. A family Bible, a massive, leather tooled tome in faded brown and gold, rests on the top of it. Just up stage of the doors, and a few feet into the room, is a leather-topped library table with a chair behind it. This is angled towards the drinks table. Opposite this, and angled towards the other small table is an Edwardian chaise-longue. The room is thickly carpeted. Wall lights provide an alternative to the central chandelier. Switches for both are by the doors. Cobwebs are festooned all over.

When the curtain rises, the room is in darkness, the only light being a faint haze from outside the french windows.

After a moment, the doors open and light from the hall spills into the room. **VERNON PREWITT** *fumbles for the light switches and flicks them on. He is apparently a stereotype homosexual from a Sixties television sitcom. Limp wristed, mincing gait and over-emphasised facial expressions, and wearing a frilly apron over powder blue chinos, loose yellow sweatshirt and a loosely knotted chiffon scarf around his neck. His hands are encased in pink rubber cleaning gloves and he carries a plastic cleaning box containing a feather duster, cloths, spray polishes and a kitchen roll. He views the room with distaste and sniffs.*

VERNON *(pulling a face)* Oh, my gawd. Smells like somebody's died in here. *(He brushes cobwebs out of his face, deposits the cleaning box on the library table and crosses to the windows)* Let's have a bit of air in the place. *(He turns the key and struggles to open them. Irritated)* Oh, come on you dozy mare. *(He flings the windows open with a gasp of triumph, takes a deep breath and almost chokes. He quickly closes them again, and reels back into the room. He gasps)* Oh, my God. *(He clutches at his throat)* It's like a whore's drawers. *(Anguished)* Ohhhhhhhh. *(He grabs a canister of air freshener from the cleaning things and sprays it heavily around before cautiously sniffing the air again)* Oh, that's better. *(He puts the canister down and gazes around the room distastefully)* Look at the state of it. All the old world charm of the average reclamation centre. *(He sighs)* The things I do to keep body and soul together. *(He picks up the feather duster)*

EDNA *(offstage)* Vernon? Are you there, Vernon?

VERNON *(calling)* In here, darlin'. Exterminating the tarantulas. *(He wafts the duster at the cobwebs)*

EDNA HONEYWILL *appears in the doorway. She is a dim-looking girl of eighteen with frizzy hair and thick round spectacles that make her look like a startled owl. She is dressed in an old-fashioned maid's costume that is obviously several sizes too large for her, black stockings and thick sensible shoes.*

Gawd, look at the size of 'em. You could put a saddle on that one and ride it to market. *(He flicks the duster)* Go on. Shoo.

EDNA *(displaying her dress)* Is this all right, do you think? It feels awfully baggy up here. *(She indicates her bust)*

VERNON Well, you know what they say, luvvie. What Nature's forgotten, just stuff with cotton. *(He eyes her up and down)* Mind you—you'd need a bolster down there to make that look as if it fit you. Haven't you got anything else?

EDNA It's what Mr Crayle left for me. *(Plaintively)* I *told* him I was size eight.

VERNON Oh, darlin'. He's so senile, that one, he probably thought you meant your *shoe* size. *(Kindly)* If I'd known it was going to be a costume do, I could have lent you that *divine* little number I wore in *La Cage aux Folles*. Black *moiré* silk, with a cinch waist and loads of white frilly petticoats. *(He glances at her thoughtfully)* Mind you...you haven't got the legs, have you? The "Courier" said mine looked as though I'd borrowed 'em from Cyd Charisse.

EDNA *(blankly)* Who?

VERNON Charisse, dear. Cyd *Charisse*. *(Dreamily)* Oooh, she had legs up to her armpits, did Cyd.

EDNA *(helpfully)* I've heard of Sid *James*.

VERNON *(rolling his eyes and muttering to himself)* Some people have got *no* sense of propriety. *(To her)* Anyway...what are you doing trying frocks on? I thought you were making the beds and things.

EDNA I have done. *And* I've put the roast in and peeled the veg. But it's no use doing anything else till everybody's here, is it?

VERNON Well, if you're standing around doing nothing, you can give me a hand in here. The dust's so thick, the spiders are having to run around on stilts. Run the vacuum over the curtains and see if you can clean 'em up a bit, but for Gawd's sake don't open the window. The smell out there's enough to choke you. Talk about your life flashing before your eyes. I was up to twenty-seven before I got it shut again. *(He fusses around, dusting)*

EDNA *(wrinkling her nose)* It's full of smells, this place. There was one in the *kitchen*. Under the floorboards. I had to use *bottles* of disinfectant to get rid of it.

VERNON *(dusting the bookcases)* Probably the drains, dear. You know what these old houses are like. *(Primly)* If you ask me, it hasn't had a good fettling since Dick's days. *(He lashes at the bookcase)* Ugh, get out, you brute. *(He shakes the duster distastefully)*

EDNA *(puzzled)* Who's Dick?

VERNON *(patiently)* *King* Dick, luvvie. *(He clarifies)* Richard the Third.

EDNA *(awed)* Was this *his* house, then?

VERNON *(wincing)* No, dear. It's an expression. It means nobody's touched it for ages. *(To himself)* And I know just how it feels. *(To her)* Look. Are you *going* to help me, or are you just going to stand there all night and watch?

EDNA *(uneasily)* I don't want to get the dress dirty. I'm supposed to make a good impression, and they'll be here any time now.

VERNON *(pouting)* Well, I'll tell you this much for nothing, dear. It's the last time *I* put myself out for the flaming agency. I'm an actress, I am, not a domestic help.

EDNA *(meekly)* But it is an emergency, Vernon. And you *were* out of work.

VERNON *(acidly)* I was resting, dear. Resting. *Ordinary* people are "out of work". *Professionals* "rest". Besides—I turned down a walk-on in *Emmerdale* for this. *(He glances out of the window and shrieks)* Oh, my God. Look at that. *(He waggles the feather duster at the window)*

EDNA *(startled)* What?

VERNON Fog, dear. *Fog.* It's coming down the drive like the Severn Bore. *(Disgustedly)* Well, that's charming, that is. Absolutely *charming*. If they get stuck in this lot, they're not going to be here till midnight. And then what's going to happen?

EDNA *(glancing at her watch)* It's only ten to seven.

VERNON And the last train to Basildon goes at half past eight. What am I going to do if they tell me to *walk* to the village? *(Petulantly)* Oooh, I hate the countryside. Who in their right mind'd want to live *here*? It's miles away from civilization and smack in the middle of a stinking *swamp*.

ZOE MAPLETON *enters in time to hear his last words. She is a hard-looking woman in her thirties, dressed in skirt and long sleeved blouse. She carries a notepad and pen.*

ZOE *(matter-of-factly)* It's not a swamp, Mr Prewitt, it's a marsh. And the type of people who live in Monument House, are those who value their privacy. Now do you have any more questions, or can we expect you to complete the work you were engaged for *before* our guests arrive?

VERNON *makes a moue, then quickly resumes his dusting.*

(to **EDNA***)* I should check the oven, if I were you, Edna. The roast smells as though it might need looking at.

EDNA *begins to exit.*

And Edna. Try to do something with the uniform. We *do* want to make a good impression, don't we?

EDNA *(breathlessly)* Yes, miss.

EDNA *drops a quick curtsy and exits.*

ZOE *looks at* **VERNON***'s back, runs a fingertip over the tabletop, then examines it.*

ZOE You won't forget to polish the furniture, will you, Mr Prewitt? I could write my name in the dust on this tabletop. *(She turns to exit)*

VERNON Yes, miss. *(He turns back to his dusting)* Snotty cow.

ZOE *(turning)* Did you say something, Mr Prewitt?

VERNON *(flustered)* I said... I'll do it now. *(He moves quickly to the table and grabs the polish and duster)*

ZOE And by the way...you *did* clean the brasswork on the main door?

VERNON *(forcing a smile)* I thought I'd leave that till *last*, Mrs Mapleton.

ZOE I see. Personally, I'd prefer to have it done *now*. Before anyone else sees it. First impressions are *so* important, don't you think?

VERNON *(pursing his lips and glowering)* Yes, Mrs Mapleton. I'll get right on to it. *(He puts down the spray polish and picks up a tin of brass cleaner, muttering)* I'll see if I can find a "Welcome" mat to put down, as well, shall I?

VERNON *exits huffily as* MORTIMER CRAYLE *enters the room.* CRAYLE *is a small man in his late seventies, gimlet eyed, and wearing a badly made hairpiece that fails to match his real colouring. He is dressed in a morning suit that would not have looked out of place in the nineteen thirties, and carries a slim grey folder in one hand.*

CRAYLE *(seeing* ZOE*)* Ah, Zoe, my dear. I was wondering where you'd got to. Is everything all right?

ZOE *(coolly)* Is there any reason why it shouldn't be?

CRAYLE No, no. Of course not. *(He moves behind her towards the drinks table)* There's very little *you'd* leave to chance, is there? I sometimes envy that devious mind of yours. *(He puts the folder down and selects a decanter)*

ZOE Coming from you, that's the joke of the century. You're so damned crooked, you have to screw your socks on.

CRAYLE *(pouring a drink)* Crooked or not, my dear, without me you wouldn't stand a chance of pulling this off, so why don't we settle our differences and behave like reasonable human beings, eh?

ZOE *(icily)* Since when did *you* start doing impersonations? *(Her composure breaking)* My God, Crayle, you've got a nerve. I'm the one who found that ledger and realized what it was. If it hadn't been for me, you'd have been doing twenty years for embezzlement by now. *(She sneers)* Penworthy, Venner and Crayle. Trusted Family Solicitors. *(She snorts)* Hah. When I think of the salary I got for practically running the place, and the amounts you three were skimming off clients accounts, I could *choke.*

CRAYLE *(lifting his glass to drink)* Perhaps—

ZOE *(snapping)* Nothing. If Judge Donnington hadn't availed himself of "certain services" back in nineteen eighty-two, and *that* old monster *(she indicates the portrait of Septimus)* hadn't recorded exactly what those services were—you'd have been done for, wouldn't you? *(Bitterly)* You can thank your lucky stars that respectability commands a very high price. *(She moves downstage left)*

CRAYLE *(sagely)* How true, my dear. How very true. As my late partner Mr Penworthy used to say—one of the most comforting things in life is the absolute knowledge that most great people are indebted to their past crimes for their present fortunes. *(He moves to the fireplace, puts down his glass, strikes a match and applies it to the fire)* But whilst admitting the truth of what you say, at the time of your discovery you were still working for the firm—and under *my* instruction. *(He picks up his glass again)* That being the case, I fail to see why we should not *both* benefit from this very fortuitous event. *(He stands with his back to the fire)*

ZOE And what if something goes *wrong*?

CRAYLE *(raising an eyebrow)* Wrong? What could possibly go wrong? They arrive, we dispose of them, and the rest is plain sailing. *(He sips his drink)*

ZOE *(tightly)* I still don't like it. It's an added complication. How could they possibly have found out what we were doing? They don't even know the account book exists.

CRAYLE *(smiling thinly)* Never underestimate the Tombs, my dear. Insane they may be, but believe *me*, they know *everything*. And unless we eliminate them quickly, there is *no chance whatsoever* of putting the contents of that book to good use.

ZOE *(shaking her head; amused)* They really scare you, don't they?

CRAYLE *(drily)* Alive, yes. For over four hundred years, they've dealt in the business of paid assassination... *(He moves down to the wing chair)* and never, in all that time, has the least breath of suspicion been directed against them. You *could* say they're unique. Perfect murder machines. Their crimes undetectable. Methods infallible. And efficiency— *(He shrugs)* unbeatable. *(He sits down)*

ZOE Then how come most of them were killed off in this place?

CRAYLE *(frowning)* Yes. I'll never understand that. It's a total mystery.

ZOE Well in *my* opinion, they got exactly what they deserved. And for what it's worth, if they *were* still around, *you* wouldn't be sitting there dribbling into your whisky. You'd be stitching mailbags, or whatever it is they do these days.

CRAYLE *(amused)* You're a hard woman, Zoe. *(He sips at his drink)*

ZOE I've good cause. *(She glances at her notepad)* I'd better check the bedrooms. *(She moves towards the door)*

CRAYLE *(musing)* You know... In some ways you remind me of Monica Tomb.

ZOE *halts and gives him an incredulous look.*

Oh—we only met a few times. The odd occasions I deputised for Penworthy during his illnesses. But all the same... *(His voice trails away into silence)*

ZOE *What?*

CRAYLE It's hard to believe that even *she* fell victim. One wonders at times if...? Well—as you know—her body was never found. *(He smiles wistfully)* I was very fond of Monica, and I flatter myself she returned the feeling.

ZOE   Really? I thought she was into nymphomania—not necrophilia.

CRAYLE *gives her a vitriolic glare.*

Did it never occur to you that *she* could have finished them all off? It did to me. Despite the results of that pathetic excuse for an inquiry.

CRAYLE *(firmly)* Not for one moment. No. Despite her past record, Monica Tomb was quite innocent of *that* particular crime.

ZOE   And what makes you so sure about that?

CRAYLE   If she *had* been the killer, there would never have *been* an inquiry. The bodies would have vanished as though they'd never existed, not been scattered about the house as they were. This whole estate is one vast charnel. The marsh alone could contain an army... *(Amused)* and probably *does*. But no amount of draining will ever persuade *that* to give up its secrets. That's why Monument House is the perfect place to bring down the curtain on the Tomb Dynasty. Once we've disposed of these final few, the world will be our oyster. *(He beams)*

ZOE   *(icily)* Just don't try to double-cross me, Crayle, or you'll regret it for the rest of your life. I want every penny of my share. Understand? Every single penny.

ZOE *exits.*

CRAYLE   *(gazing after her)* Don't worry, my dear. You'll get everything you deserve. I can personally guarantee it. *(He chuckles mirthlessly and sips his drink, then reaching around, he takes the folder from the table and looks at it thoughtfully)* Oh, what a tangled web we weave, when first we practise to deceive. *(Putting his glass down on the table, he opens the folder, takes out a thin sheaf of typewritten papers and peruses them in satisfaction)* Septimus... Lucien... Dora... Emily... Marcus... Oliver... Monica... All deceased.

(He beams) And now for the final few. *(He chuckles)* The final few.

VERNON *enters huffily with his polish and duster.*

VERNON Right. Well that's that done. She can see her rotten face in the brasswork, and I hope it gives her a heart attack. *(He sees* CRAYLE *and reacts)* Oh. *(He winces)* Sorry, Mr Crayle. I didn't realize you were still here. *(He drops the duster and polish into the cleaning box and picks it up quickly)* I'll do the room next door, shall I? I can finish off in here later. *(He turns to exit)*

CRAYLE *(sharply)* Mr Prewitt...

VERNON *stops dead in his tracks. As he does so, there is a hammering at the main door, off.*

VERNON *(relieved)* Oh...sounds like your visitors have arrived. *(Helpfully)* Would you like *me* to get it?

CRAYLE *(hastily)* No. No. *(He stuffs the papers back into the folder)* We won't keep you any longer. Just collect your things and be on your way.

VERNON *(surprised)* But what about the cleaning? I've still got next door to do, and I haven't finished in here, yet.

CRAYLE No matter. I'll ask the girl to finish off.

VERNON *(flustered)* But—

CRAYLE Don't worry. You'll receive your full salary. Goodbye, Mr Prewitt. And thank you for your assistance.

VERNON *(nonplussed)* Oh. *(He shrugs)* Well. I'll get my things, then.

Before he can move, EDNA *enters.*

EDNA *(announcing)* Miss Octavia Tomb, sir.

She drops an awkward curtsy and steps aside to allow OCTAVIA TOMB *to enter.* OCTAVIA *is in her sixties,*

*aristocratic, gaunt, deathly pale, and her iron grey hair
is scraped back into a bun into which two large steel
pins are embedded, reminiscent of Widow Twankey in
Aladdin. She wears steel-rimmed spectacles, but her eyes
miss nothing. She is dressed in black chiffon, with jet
beads and accessories.*

CRAYLE *(beaming)* My dear Miss Tomb. *(He extends his hand
and moves towards her)* Mortimer Crayle. The Family
Solicitor.

OCTAVIA *(quickly holding up her hand to silence him)* Hush.
Hush.

He stops dead in his tracks.

(cocking her head as though listening) I need to hear them.

VERNON *and* EDNA *exchange glances.*

CRAYLE *(frowning)* Hear them?

OCTAVIA The voices, Mr Crayle. The voices of those who perished
within these walls. *(Almost whispering)* Can't you hear
them? Crying out to us. *(Dramatically)* For *vengeance.*

VERNON *and* EDNA *exchange glances again.*

VERNON *(hastily)* Well—I'd better be going then. *(He moves
towards the door)*

OCTAVIA *(imperiously)* Wait.

VERNON *comes to a halt.*

(turning to face him) And who are you?

VERNON *(with false brightness)* Oh, nobody important. Just
the cleaner.

OCTAVIA *(eyes narrowing)* The *cleaner. (She moves closer
to him)* Ah, yes. There's something there. In your *aura.*
Something—familiar...elusive...*tantalising. (She closes her*

eyes and takes a deep dramatic breath) What is it? *(With great emphasis)* What is it?

VERNON *(nervously)* "Obsession" ... With just a splash of "Kouros".

OCTAVIA *(eyes snapping open) Blood.* I see *blood* on this man's hands.

Everyone looks at VERNON's *hands.*

VERNON *(hastily)* Oh, no. No. These are just cleaning gloves. They're pink, you see. *Pink. (He shows them)* I couldn't get Marigolds.

OCTAVIA *(sucking in a breath) A reading.* I *must* do a reading. *(To* EDNA) Quickly. My travelling bag. Bring me the Tarot cards.

EDNA *gapes at her.*

CRAYLE *(interrupting)* I'm afraid there's no time, Miss Tomb. Mr Prewitt is about to leave.

VERNON *(hastily)* Yes. I've got a train to catch. To Basildon. But it was *lovely* meeting you. *(He edges to the door)* Have a nice weekend.

VERNON *exits quickly, leaving* OCTAVIA *staring after him.*

CRAYLE *(oozing charm)* May I...offer you a drink, Miss Tomb? A little sherry, perhaps?

There is no response.

(insistently) Miss Tomb?

She looks at him strangely.

Sherry?

OCTAVIA *(snapping out of her trance)* No, thank you. I never touch alcohol. It blurs the vibrations. *(More firmly)* A little herb tea, I think. *(She sits on the* chaise*)*

EDNA *(apologetically)* Oh, I don't think we've got any of *that*, miss. Not that I know of.

CRAYLE Perhaps a quick check, my dear? *(He motions her to leave)*

EDNA *gives a nervous smile and exits.*

(to **OCTAVIA***; anxiously)* You—er—arrived *alone*, Miss Tomb. Were the others not on the train?

OCTAVIA *(staring at him)* Train, Mr Crayle? I have not travelled by train since nineteen sixty-seven. I find them inconvenient, dirty, expensive, unreliable—and extremely hazardous to one's health.

CRAYLE Hazardous?

OCTAVIA Most definitely. Whilst journeying with a companion a number of years ago, he fell through an unlatched door on the nine fifty-two from Paddington. I shall never forget that experience as long as I live. *(She shudders at the memory)*

CRAYLE *(sympathetically)* I can well believe it. To see someone die before your very eyes.

OCTAVIA Die? He didn't *die*. He suffered nothing more serious than minor cuts and bruising. Had it not been for an unexpected embolism three days later, we might well have had to return the fee. *(She shakes her head)* No, Mr Crayle, I shall never place my trust in railways again. These days my dear little Porsche nine hundred eleven is sufficient to get me around.

CRAYLE You—er—still carry on the family "tradition", Miss Tomb? *(He sits)*

OCTAVIA Naturally. Though I must say much of the pleasure has gone. *(Bitterly)* Finesse is no longer appreciated. All clients require these days is instant gratification. *(Firmly)* In my opinion, there are far too many *amateurs* intruding on the scene.

CRAYLE *(smiling)* You're perfectly right, of course. But even amateurs have their moments. Particularly when following the examples of *masters*.

OCTAVIA *(coldly)* I hope I live to see the day when an amateur rises to *Tomb* standards, Mr Crayle.

CRAYLE *(smiling)* Perhaps you will, Miss Tomb. Perhaps you will.

VERNON *enters, tight-lipped, and now wearing a blouson, matching wide-brimmed hat and a long mohair scarf. He is carrying a shoulder bag.*

VERNON *(heavily)* Excuse *me,* but could somebody tell me where the taxi's parked? I've been wandering around outside for the last five minutes and that fog's playing *havoc* with my bronchials.

CRAYLE *(rising)* It appears that Miss Tomb drove herself here, Mr Prewitt, and the taxi bringing the others has not yet arrived. Perhaps you'd care to wait in the hall whilst we finish our conversation?

EDNA *enters with a scrap of paper.*

EDNA *(breathlessly)* I've found some herbs, miss. Which would you like? *(She looks at the paper and reads)* There's Bryony and Tansy, Hellebore and Celandine, Larkspur and Rowan, Foxglove and Hemlock, or Belladonna and Monkshood. *(She remembers)* Oh. And there's a little bit of Lapsang Souchong, whatever *that* is, but it smells a bit funny to me, so I wouldn't recommend it.

OCTAVIA *(after a momentary pause)* Perhaps a glass of water will suffice.

EDNA *(bobbing)* Yes, miss. *(She turns to exit)*

CRAYLE *(suddenly)* Oh, Edna. Did you bring up the wines I suggested?

EDNA *(uneasily)* You mean—the ones from down there? In the cellar?

CRAYLE Yes.

EDNA *(hanging her head in shame)* It's ever so creepy, Mr Crayle. Most of the light bulbs have gone and there's all those rusty suits of armour leaning against the walls. I'm scared there might be a man inside one of 'em.

VERNON *(aside)* She should be so lucky.

CRAYLE *(reasonably)* But we can't serve dinner without wine— now can we?

EDNA *(blinking back tears)* No, Mr Crayle.

CRAYLE So what are we going to do?

VERNON *(taking EDNA's arm)* Come on, darlin'. *I'll* go with you. I've got nothing better to do for the next few minutes anyway, and I've had *plenty* of experience in groping round in dark places.

VERNON *and* EDNA *exit.*

(offstage) I hope there's no rats down there. I can't stand rats.

OCTAVIA *(gazing after them thoughtfully)* There's something *strange* about that man. His aura disturbs the spirits.

CRAYLE *(lightly)* Oh, I'm sure there's some mistake, Miss Tomb. He's merely a *cleaner.* Once he leaves Monument House, you'll never hear of him again.

OCTAVIA *(firmly)* The spirits are never wrong, Mr Crayle. *(Thoughtfully)* Perhaps I'd better make *certain.* Fortunately I am always prepared for emergencies. *(She extracts one of her steel hair-pins and gazes at it lovingly)* You see? So slender. So delicate. So sharp. And so very, very, *(she makes a violent stabbing motion)* useful. *(She smiles insanely)*

There is a hammering at the main door.

CRAYLE *(rising hastily)* That must be the others. Excuse me.

CRAYLE *hurries out.*

OCTAVIA *replaces the pin in her hair, and smooths her dress.*

(offstage) Come in. Come in. Such a terrible evening.

There is a babbling of voices from the hall.

(offstage) How nice to meet you again. It's been a long time. Let me take your coats. Thank you. Thank you. Miss Octavia's arrived already. She's waiting in the library. Go straight through. I'll be with you in a moment.

HENRIETTA TOMB *enters the room. She is a stout woman in her mid-fifties, wearing heavy tweeds, cashmere sweater, pearls, sensible shoes and a permanent scowl.*

OCTAVIA *(primly)* Good evening, Henrietta.

HENRIETTA *(sneering)* I should have known *you'd* arrive first. Bad news always did travel fast.

OCTAVIA I do live somewhat *closer,* my dear. It must have been much more tiring for *you.* Your skin's even greyer than usual. *(Sweetly)* Why don't you sit down? I'm sure there's *something* strong enough to support you.

HENRIETTA At least I've got *flesh* on my bones. To look at you, anyone would think we were in the middle of a famine.

OCTAVIA And to look at *you,* dear, they'd think *you* were the cause of it.

HENRIETTA *(sourly)* Go boil your head. *(She crosses to the drinks table)* Is any of this safe, or is it all Dora's? *(She picks up a decanter)*

OCTAVIA *(primly)* I really couldn't say. Unlike *some* members of this family, I am not an alcoholic.

HENRIETTA *(throwing her a sour glance, then unstoppering the decanter and sniffing)* Smells all right to me.

OCTAVIA In that case, it's probably poisoned. Dora was *very* predictable.

As **HENRIETTA** *replaces the stopper,* **AUGUSTUS TOMB** *enters the room, followed by his sister* **ATHENE.** **AUGUSTUS** *is a bearded and pompous individual in his mid-fifties wearing a monocle, Norfolk jacket, knickerbockers and leggings. He speaks in loud, booming tones.* **ATHENE** *is a few years older, fluttery and highly strung, dressed in grey chiffon with pink accessories.*

AUGUSTUS *(curtly)* Good evening, Octavia.

OCTAVIA *(equally frosty)* Augustus. Athene.

ATHENE *(happily)* Oh, isn't it wonderful, Tavie? To be here in the family home again. *(She gazes around)* Such lovely, lovely memories.

HENRIETTA *(glowering)* Speak for yourself, pea-brain. *(She picks up* **CRAYLE**'s *folder and looks at it curiously)*

ATHENE *(surprised)* But I do, Henrietta. I *do.* *(Fondly)* It was here...in this very room...where Dora and I were sitting when Aunt Minerva fell down stairs and broke her neck. *(Dreamily)* I'll never forget her scream. It was *wonderful.* I'm sure she had perfect pitch.

    HENRIETTA *pulls out a few papers and glances at them.*

AUGUSTUS *(irritated)* For Heaven's sake, Athene. It's a good job Fabia hasn't arrived yet. The woman *was* her mother, you know.

ATHENE *(reasonably)* But she was only an outsider, Augustus. It wasn't as if she were *real* family. *(Petulantly)* And besides... the trip-wire wasn't *meant* for her. Monica had left it there for Emily. She'd no right to go falling over it. It spoiled the weekend for everybody.

HENRIETTA *(drily)* Not to mention *her*. *(She continues to peruse the papers)*

AUGUSTUS *(firmly)* All the same, we shall not refer to Aunt Minerva whilst Fabia is present. Is that understood?

ATHENE *(meekly)* Yes, Augustus.

OCTAVIA *(cutting in)* You're quite sure she *will* be joining us?

AUGUSTUS *(grandly)* Of course I am. Why shouldn't she?

OCTAVIA *(caustically)* She hasn't exactly kept in touch since Minerva died, has she? None of us have seen her in years.

AUGUSTUS That's precisely why she'll come. *(Proudly)* We are the *last* of the Tombs. And if the family business is to continue—which it must—everyone has to play their part. This ridiculous enmity between us will cease. We shall work for the common cause—that of upholding the Tomb tradition. Is that clearly understood?

HENRIETTA *(replacing the papers and putting the folder down again)* If you think I'm going to start holding hands with Mystic Meg, there, *(she indicates* OCTAVIA*)* you've got another think coming. I work on my *own*, I do. Always have done and always will. *(She moves to the wing chair and sits)*

AUGUSTUS *(firmly)* You'll do as you're told, Henrietta. The family's reputation is far more important than the feelings of the individual. If *I* say we work together, we *do* so. All five of us.

ATHENE *(quickly)* Six, Augustus. *Six.*

Everyone stares at her.

(defensively) We mustn't forget Aunt Vesta.

AUGUSTUS *(shocked)* Vesta.

HENRIETTA *(stunned)* Vesta.

OCTAVIA *(rising and trembling with fury)* How dare you mention that woman's name in *my* presence!

ATHENE She's still one of the family.

OCTAVIA *(weakly)* Oh, my God. *(She staggers to the drinks table, shakily lifts the first decanter and pours a drink)*

HENRIETTA *(to* **ATHENE***)* You really *have* flipped your lid, haven't you?

AUGUSTUS *(taking a firm grip on himself)* We do not mention that name in polite company, Athene.

ATHENE *(defiantly)* Well I *like* her. She taught me to play roulette.

HENRIETTA Pity it wasn't the *Russian* version. Listen, dimwits, as far as *we're* concerned, she doesn't exist. Never did and never will.

ATHENE But she does. She does. And if we don't ask *her* to join us, who's going to carry on the business when *we're* all gone?

AUGUSTUS *(snapping)* Don't be ridiculous, Athene. She'll be dead long before we are.

ATHENE *She* may be, yes. But what about her family?

HENRIETTA *(blankly)* Family? *(She glances at* **AUGUSTUS** *and* **OCTAVIA** *in question)*

OCTAVIA *is now clutching an empty glass.*

ATHENE Her little *boy*... *(She frowns)* or was it a girl? Oh, dear, I *wish* I could remember.

HENRIETTA *(gaping)* Vesta had a *baby*?

OCTAVIA *(moaning softly)* Oh, my God. *(She quickly pours another drink)*

AUGUSTUS *(shaken)* It's impossible. I don't believe it. I *won't* believe it. *(Firmly)* How do you know this?

ATHENE Oliver told me. Just after he went peculiar and thought he was a werewolf. *(Fondly)* They used to have really long talks when she took him out on his leash. It was Vesta who showed him how to howl properly...and *he* showed her... well...quite a lot of things.

HENRIETTA But what about this *baby*? Was it...normal?

ATHENE *(indignantly)* Of course it was. As normal as any of *us*. *(She frowns)* But what *was* it...? *(She struggles to remember)*

AUGUSTUS *(icily)* Never mind what it was. Why haven't you told us this before?

ATHENE *(defensively)* Because everyone gets so cross when her name's mentioned. *(Sulkily)* And besides—it was a secret.

HENRIETTA *(in disbelief)* I always knew you were a devious old cow, but— *(Suddenly)* Just a minute. Just a minute. Vesta's over ninety by now...so how old *is* this kid of hers? Fifty? Sixty?

ATHENE *(shrugging)* I suppose so. It's probably married with a family of its own, by now. *(Sadly)* A family of Tombs we may never even meet.

OCTAVIA *(faintly)* Could we please change the subject? I'm not feeling very well. *(She moves back to the chaise and sits clutching her glass)*

AUGUSTUS *(firmly)* Octavia's right. We want nothing to do with *that* branch of the family, and I forbid you to mention it ever again. We shall have no dealings with them whatsoever. Is that understood, Athene?

ATHENE *(protesting)* Oh, but Augustus—

AUGUSTUS *(thundering)* Is that understood?

ATHENE *(meekly)* Yes, Augustus.

CRAYLE *and* ZOE *enter.*

CRAYLE *(to the* TOMBS*)* So sorry to have kept you. May I introduce my secretary, Mrs Mapleton? *(He indicates to*

ZOE) Miss Octavia Tomb, Miss Athene, Miss Henrietta, and Doctor Augustus.

All acknowledge each other.

(to the TOMBS*)* Mrs Mapleton has been arranging your rooms, so if you'd care to follow her, she'll see you're all settled in comfortably. We'll have dinner as soon as Miss Fabia arrives.

HENRIETTA *and* OCTAVIA *rise to exit.*

(to OCTAVIA*)* I see you changed your mind. Shall I take the glass?

OCTAVIA *(blankly)* Glass? *(She follows his gaze to the glass she holds, blinks, then looks at the drinks table before looking back to the glass again. Realization hits her and she clutches at her throat, her face a mask of horror)*

CRAYLE *(quickly)* It's quite all right, Miss Octavia. I personally re-stocked every decanter on the table. Just in case of "accidents". *(He takes the glass)* Thank you.

OCTAVIA *composes herself.* HENRIETTA *looks amused.* ATHENE *and* AUGUSTUS *look sympathetic.*

ZOE *(to the* TOMBS*)* If you'll come this way.

ZOE *exits, followed by the* TOMBS.

CRAYLE *crosses to the drinks table and puts the glass down.*

EDNA *enters in some concern; her apron, hands, and face, streaked with dust and grime.*

EDNA *(anxiously)* Oh, Mr Crayle, sir. Mr Crayle. *(Her hands flap)*

CRAYLE *(turning to her)* Yes? *(He notes her state)* Is something wrong?

EDNA It's Mr Prewitt, sir. Vernon. He's had an accident. Down in the cellars. *(She glances off, concernedly)*

CRAYLE *(sharply)* Accident?

EDNA We were just coming back with the wine when he tripped up and nearly put his foot in one of those great big rat-traps they've got down there. You know. The ones about this size— *(She holds her hands about two feet apart)* with horrible rusty teeth and chained to the floor. And anyway... he fell sideways into some sort of cage and the door bounced back and locked itself. I've been trying to get him out for ages but it won't budge. *(She bites her lip)*

CRAYLE *(fuming)* Blast the man. *(To her)* There, there, my dear. Nothing to get upset about. Mrs Mapleton has keys to every lock in the house. We'll have Mr Prewitt free in no time. Just—tidy yourself up a little and I'll go find her. *(He heads for the door, then pauses)* If our last guest arrives, I'll be back in a few minutes.

CRAYLE *exits.*

EDNA *pulls out a handkerchief and brushes ineffectually at the grime on her uniform and hands.*

EDNA *(miserably)* Oh, look at the state I'm in. I look like a chimney sweep. I'm never going to get this clean before dinner.

There is a loud hammering at the main door which startles her. Quickly she tugs her uniform into a semblance of neatness and puts her handkerchief away.

(calling) Coming.

EDNA *hurries out into the hall and a moment or two later gives a scream of terror.*

LARRY *(offstage; anxiously)* It's all right. It's all right. It's just me. I mean... I'm harmless. I'm sorry. I'm sorry. It's all right. Honestly.

EDNA *(offstage; fighting hysteria)* What do you want?

LARRY *(offstage; quickly)* To get help. For the van. I've had an accident, you see. In the fog. A crash.

EDNA *(annoyed)* Well what do you want to go walking round like *that* for? I nearly had a heart attack. *(Suspiciously)* You've not got any animals with you, have you?

LARRY *(offstage)* What?

EDNA *(offstage)* Elephants and things.

LARRY *(offstage)* Oh, no. No. Look...can I come in? It's a bit cold out here and this is all I've got on. Thank you. Oh...sorry about the mud. I think I walked into a bog, or something. Do you think—

EDNA *(offstage)* You'd better come through to the library. Mr Crayle's gone looking for his secretary but he'll be back in a minute. *(After a slight pause)* Have you hurt your leg?

LARRY *(offstage)* Just banged it, I think. Nothing broken. But it looks like the van's a complete write off.

EDNA *enters the room, followed by a limping* **LARRY LEWISS.** *He is a young man of twenty-five or so, but totally unrecognizable in his guise as a circus clown. White-faced with black arched eyebrows, fake eyelashes, huge red lips, rouged cheekbones, and a flesh nose-tip where his red nose would be. A garish hat with a huge daisy trim is atop a curly bright coloured wig, his body encased in a baggy, zany clown suit which is mud-splattered and wet from the knees down, and his feet are in muddy outsized boots.*

EDNA You still haven't said why you're dressed up like that.

LARRY *(awkwardly)* Oh. Yes. Well. I'm a children's entertainer, you see. Balloon sculpture and magic and all that sort of thing. You might have heard of me? Cough-drop the Clown. *(He strikes a pose)*

EDNA *(blankly)* No.

LARRY *(disconcerted)* Oh. *(Brightly)* Well. I dress up like this when I'm doing gigs. That's—er—kiddies parties and carnivals, etc. I've been doing one over in Bradwell. A birthday party.

EDNA *(frowning)* And don't you get changed when you've finished?

LARRY *(quickly)* Oh, yes. Yes. Normally, I do. But I've got another one in Burnham in an hour's time—and I was running late, so I left everything on and hoped I wouldn't get stopped for speeding. *(He grimaces)* Speeding. Huh. First I took a wrong turning, then I got stuck behind a tractor, and then I hit this fog. That's how I crashed the van. I was coming round the bend at the bottom of the drive, when a taxi shot out in front of me and went tearing down the road like a bat out of hell. I swerved to avoid him, ran up the banking, bounced off a tree trunk and toppled straight into the gatepost. It's a wonder I wasn't killed. The drive's completely blocked, and the van's an absolute write off. So now I need the phone to get help.

EDNA *(uncertainly)* I don't think there *is* a phone. I mean—there is one, but it's not working. We only came in this morning and nobody's lived here for ages.

LARRY *(disbelievingly)* You mean...you can't call the AA or anything? You're stuck in the middle of nowhere?

EDNA *(nodding)* We haven't even got real electricity. Just one of those generator things behind the house.

LARRY *(despairingly)* Oh, that's marvellous. Just what I needed. What am I going to do now? *(He sits on the* chaise*)*

EDNA *(helpfully)* There's a phone in the village. It's only a few miles down the road.

LARRY In Haslow, you mean? Yes. I saw it on the signpost. But I don't know that I can walk there with this leg. It's starting to hurt like crazy. *(He feels gingerly at the lower* *part of his leg and winces)* Ow ow ow. *(He begins to pull up his trouser leg)*

EDNA *(suddenly)* You could go in the taxi. The one that's supposed to be taking Vernon. He should have gone in the other one...the one that made you crash...but he's down in the cellar at the minute, locked in a cage.

LARRY Oh. Taking him to the vet, are you?

EDNA *(blankly)* Vet? *(She realizes)* Oh, no. No. *(She giggles)* He's not a dog or anything. He's the *cleaner.* We work for the same agency...except for when he's *starring.* He's really famous in Basildon, is Vernon. Does all the leads with the Operatic Society, *and* he's done walk-ons twice for television.

LARRY *(curiously)* So...what's he doing locked in a cage?

EDNA Well...

There is a hammering at the main door.

(startled) Oh. That'll be the taxi. Just wait there and I'll be back in a minute.

EDNA *exits.*

LARRY *(rising)* But it can't be. I've just explained. There's no way... *(He realizes he is too late, shrugs, and sits again despondently)*

FABIA *(offstage)* Hallo, darlin'. Innit a night, eh? Sorry I'm late but—

EDNA *(offstage; hastily)* 'Scuse me, miss. I've got to stop the taxi.

FABIA *(offstage)* Stop the taxi? You'll have to get a move on, darlin'. He'll be halfway home, by now. Oh, well. Please yourself. *(She calls brightly)* Yoo-hoo. Anybody home?

A moment later, **FABIA TOMB** *enters the room. She is a busty blonde in her early forties, slightly overweight and struggling to keep herself decently covered by a suit at least four sizes too small for her. She appears*

*to be encrusted with diamond jewellery, totters about
in extra-high heeled shoes, and wears a thick fur coat
over her outfit. She carries a large flashy handbag. In
contrast to the other* TOMBs, *she is giggly, flirtatious
and loud in every sense of the word.*

(seeing LARRY*)* Oh, my God. It's Ronald McDonald. *(She
laughs coarsely)* Nobody told me it was fancy dress. *(To*
LARRY*)* Hello, darlin'.

LARRY *begins to rise.*

No, no. Don't get up. Not unless you're going to do a spot
of juggling. *(She laughs again)* Who are *you*, then? Not
Mortimer Crayle, that's for sure. *(She dumps her bag on the
library table and shrugs off her coat)* Never met a solicitor
yet with a sense of humour. *(She introduces herself)* Fabia
Tomb, darlin'. The youngest and prettiest. *(She settles herself
next to him)*

LARRY   Er... Larry Lewiss. I'm an entertainer.

FABIA   *(archly)* Ooooh. You can entertain *me* any time, love.
(She winks at him) So what's *your* story?

LARRY   *(blankly)* I beg your pardon?

FABIA   Who do you want bumped off, love? Ringmaster...or a
couple of Liberty Horses. *(She laughs and slaps* LARRY's
thigh) Don't be shy. We're all friends in this place. *(Archly)*
Leastways, I hope we are. *(She squeezes his leg)*

LARRY   *(squirming)* I don't know what you mean.

FABIA   Course you do. *(Archly)* I bet you're quite a looker under
that lot, aren't you? Well, you scratch *my* back, darlin' and
I'll scratch anything you want scratching. *(She laughs loudly)*
So come on. Tell Aunty Fabia. Who's been upsetting you?
(She edges closer to him)

LARRY   *(uncomfortably)* Nobody. I had an accident. At the
bottom of the drive—

FABIA You mean—that's *your* van that's wrapped round the gateposts?

LARRY *(nodding)* I'm afraid so.

FABIA *(playfully)* Oooh, you naughty boy. I *wondered* who it was who'd blocked me passage. *(She laughs coarsely)* I've a good mind to slap your wrist, I have. I had to walk half a mile up that drive in my best shoes. And in thick fog. Good job I knew the way, else I might have ended up at the bottom of the marsh with all the other nosey sods who pushed their luck too far. *(She beams)* Still—I'm here now, and that's all that matters, isn't it? *(She grips his knee again)*

LARRY *(gulping)* Not for me. I'm supposed to be doing a performance in half an hour, but there's not a hope of getting there now.

FABIA *(kindly)* Never mind, darlin'. You can stay here and do a performance for me. I've always fancied fellers in show business. Fell for a trapeze artiste once, but it didn't last long. *(She nudges him)* His wife came home unexpected, like, and caught us in the act. *(She laughs uproariously)*

CRAYLE *hurries into the room.*

LARRY *stands.*

CRAYLE *(breathlessly)* My dear Miss Tomb. So sorry... *(He sees* **LARRY** *and falters)* to have kept you. *(Confusedly)* A slight problem in the cellar. *(He pulls himself together)* Mortimer Crayle. Family Solicitor.

FABIA *(cheerfully)* That's all right, dear. We won't hold it against you. *(She laughs)* No need to get your knickers in a twist. This gentleman's been keeping me entertained. *(She indicates* **LARRY***)*

LARRY Larry Lewiss. Children's entertainer. *(He extends his hand)*

CRAYLE *(ignoring it and speaking to* **FABIA***)* Then...you're not *together?*

FABIA *(archly)* Give us a chance, darlin'. I've only just met him. *(She laughs)* No. He's crashed his van and blocked the drive. I had to walk up here from the road. Look at the state of my shoes. *(She extends her feet for inspection)* Two hundred quid, these cost me. *(To LARRY, cheerfully)* Don't worry about it, dear. It's only money and I'm not short of a bob or two. *(She winks at him)*

CRAYLE *(incredulous)* You mean the drive's impassable?

LARRY *(apologetically)* I'm afraid so. Yes.

CRAYLE *(to LARRY; coldly)* So what are you doing here?

LARRY I came to use the phone...but the maid said you weren't connected. She said I might be able to share a taxi back to the village, but of course, the taxi couldn't get through, could it, so... *(Defeated)* I seem to be out of luck. Looks like I'll have to walk it.

CRAYLE Indeed it does. I'll show you out, shall I? *(He indicates the hall)*

LARRY *begins to limp towards the door.*

FABIA *(rising)* Oh, come on, Morty. He can't walk there like that. The poor lamb's half drowned—*and* he's got a bad leg.

LARRY *(pausing)* Oh, it's nothing. Just bruised a bit. I'll manage.

FABIA *(firmly)* You'll do no such thing. I'm not having you developing blood clots and gangrene from walking round on a poorly leg. There's plenty of beds in this place. You can spend the night here and we'll sort out your other problems tomorrow. All right?

LARRY *(quickly)* Oh, no. I couldn't. Really. I mean...

FABIA Course you can. I insist. *(She pulls him back to the chaise)*

CRAYLE *(clearly annoyed)* If you don't mind my saying so, Miss Tomb...we have *family business* to discuss.

FABIA *(settling herself down)* So?

CRAYLE *(tightly)* I hardly think the presence of an *outsider* will be conducive to frank exchanges between beneficiaries.

FABIA *(frowning)* Blimey. Have you swallowed a dictionary? *(Sweetly)* Listen, darlin'. He'll be staying one night. Tonight. And tomorrow morning, he'll be gone. We've got the rest of the weekend to discuss business. All right?

LARRY *(nervously)* Look. I don't want...

FABIA *(cutting in)* Neither do I, love. You're staying. *(She pulls him down beside her)*

EDNA *enters in a fluster.*

EDNA *(to* CRAYLE*)* Oh, sir. It's Vernon. He's getting himself into a right state about missing his train. It's a quarter to eight now, and he'll never get to the station for half past.

FABIA *(looking at* CRAYLE*)* Vernon?

CRAYLE *(testily)* The cleaner I employed. He should have left ages ago. *(To* LARRY*)* This is your fault, you idiot.

EDNA *(plaintively)* What's he going to do, sir?

CRAYLE *(snapping)* How the devil should I know?

FABIA *(cheerfully)* Only one thing he can do, isn't there? *He'll* have to stay the night as well.

CRAYLE *(outraged)* But that's totally out of the question. I couldn't possibly allow it.

FABIA Course you couldn't, darlin'. But *I* could. And seeing as how I'm part *owner* of this place, I think I'm entitled to decide what guests I'm going to have. All right? *(To* EDNA*)* Find a couple of rooms for 'em, darlin'. *And* extra places for dinner.

EDNA *(looking doubtfully at* CRAYLE *then back to* FABIA*)* Yes, Miss. *(To* LARRY*)* Would you like to come this way, sir?

LARRY *(embarrassed)* Look...

FABIA *(pushing him up)* Off you go, darlin'. Get that slap off your face and clean yourself up. I'll see you later. *(She winks at him)*

LARRY *reluctantly follows* EDNA *into the hall and they vanish from sight.*

CRAYLE *(fuming)* This is most unwise, Miss Fabia.

FABIA *(easily)* I know. But it'd be a damn sight more unwise to let him go. You see... I thought he was a customer when I arrived, and let the cat out of the bag. He hasn't had time to think about it yet, but when he *does*...well...we can't afford to take chances, can we?

CRAYLE You mean?

FABIA Oh, yes. We'll have to get rid of him. Shame really. He seems quite a nice young man. But there it is.

CRAYLE And...what about the others? Prewitt and the girl.

FABIA *gives him a look.*

Yes. Yes. Of course. No witnesses. *(Suddenly)* But the agency who sent them. They know they're here.

FABIA *(rising)* Course they do, darlin'. *(She moves to the table to collect her things)* But it's a foggy night...and if Mr Lewiss offers to give them a lift to the station in his van and drives into the marsh by mistake, *we* ain't going to know a thing about it till somebody reports 'em all missing, are we? And who's to say they'll ever be found? *(She shakes her head)* Breaks yer bleedin' heart, it does.

CRAYLE *(slowly)* Yes. Yes. So...when do you propose to act?

FABIA Oh, not till the *mornin'*, dear. It's a chilly night, and I always did prefer warm flesh to a hot water bottle. See you at dinner.

FABIA *laughs coarsely, winks and exits.*

CRAYLE *watches her out of sight, then moves to the internal phone and punches a button. After listening for a moment, he breaks the connection and tries another number. Again, there is no reply. He replaces the receiver, and stands in thought, then moving to the doors, he closes them. Moving to the bookcase on the left of the fireplace he opens the secret panel to reveal a dark passageway. Vanishing into it, he re-emerges a moment later with a tray of duplicate decanters to the ones on the table. Crossing to the drinks table, he substitutes them for the ones on his tray, then looks at the fresh decanters with satisfaction. He then carries the tray of old decanters back into the passage, re-emerges and closes the entrance.*

The internal phone buzzes. He hurries down and picks up the receiver.

CRAYLE   Crayle. *(He pauses)* Ah, Zoe, my dear. I tried to reach you a moment ago. Is everything all right? *(He listens)* Good. Good. *(He listens)* Yes, I know. There was nothing I could do about it. But it doesn't matter. We go ahead as planned and dispose of all of them. Now listen. The change-over is done. Every decanter is poisoned and with any luck, they'll be dead by midnight. What? *(He listens)* Yes. I know that. Just leave Octavia to me. I've something rather special in mind for her. *(He smiles and replaces the receiver)*

The buzzer sounds almost at once and he picks up the receiver again.

(smiling broadly) Ah, it's you, my dear. I was wondering if you'd... *(He listens and chuckles)* But of course it is. Just as I promised. By this time tomorrow, everything will be ours. *(Airily)* Oh, there'll be the additional bodies to contend with, of course, but I'm sure you'll agree that they will be no problem. *(He chuckles, then suddenly scowls)* Certainly not. We do exactly as agreed. Exactly. Do I make myself clear? *(He listens)*

Behind him, the secret panel begins to open.

(cooing) No, no, Pussycat. Of course I'm not cross with you. It's just that we have to be *careful.* If the others even *suspected* what we were up to... *(He listens)* Very well. But I have to go now. There are still some minor details that need attention. I'll see you at dinner. *(He blows a kiss into the receiver, replaces it, then becomes aware that the panel is open. He turns quickly to face it)* Who's there? Who is it?

There is silence. Cautiously he approaches the opening.

Zoe? Is that you?

He steps into the passageway and vanishes from sight.

(offstage) Is anyone there? *(Startled) You.* What are *you* doing here? *(Sharply)* No. Keep away from me. You can't *do* this. *(He screeches)* No.

His cry is silenced by the sound of a dull thud. A few seconds later, the panel softly closes.

There is a timid knock on the library door. After a moment it is repeated and **EDNA** *enters.*

EDNA Shall I start dinner now, sir? *(She sees the room is empty)* Oh. Now where's *he* got to? Talk about vanishing tricks.

EDNA *turns off the lights as she exits and closes the door behind her.*

Once more the room is dark but for the glow of the fire.

Scene Two

The same. Fifteen minutes later.

The room is still in semi-darkness.

After a moment, the doors open and ZOE *appears in the opening. Light spills in from the hall.*

ZOE *(uncertainly)* Crayle? *(She flicks on the lights and looks round. Tightly)* Damn. *(She is about to leave when she catches sight of the folder on the table. Swiftly she crosses to it, snatches it up and quickly checks the contents. Grimly)* The imbecile. If any of them had seen this... *(Frustrated)* Where the hell is he?

VERNON *flounces into the room, a peevish expression on his face. He has shed his outdoor clothing.*

VERNON *(huffily)* Excuse me.

ZOE *starts, and quickly turns to face him.*

But seeing as how I'm stuck here for the night, do you want me to carry on, or what?

ZOE *(distractedly)* I'm sorry?

VERNON *(patiently)* The cleaning. I never got finished in here, and there's still next door to do.

ZOE *(pulling herself together)* You'd better speak to Mr Crayle about it.

VERNON *(tartly)* If I could find him, dear, I *would* do. I've been looking for the past ten minutes.

ZOE *(irritated)* Then please yourself. Just—keep out of the way and don't bother the guests.

ZOE *crosses in front of him and exits.*

VERNON *(caustically)* Well, thank you, Joan Crawford. And give my regards to Baby Jane. *(Waspishly)* In that case, dearie, you can stuff your cleaning. I've been on my feet since eight o'clock this morning and it's time I had a sit down. *(He crosses to the wing chair, muttering)* No wonder I'm feeling fragile. I've got stomach ulcers the size of dinner plates and I've had nothing to eat all day but slices of overdone pizza. *(He sits)* And she ought to know by now I can't *stand* anchovies. *(He leans back and closes his eyes)* Oooh, that's better.

The secret panel opens silently behind him and a frowning ATHENE *enters from the passage clutching a blood-stained meat cleaver. As the panel closes behind her, she notices* VERNON. *For a moment she studies him, moving closer for a better view. Suddenly she beams, and face aglow with expectation taps him on the shoulder.*

(irritated) What? *(He opens his eyes to see her and reacts)* Aghhhhh. *(He scrambles madly out of the chair and backs away from her)*

ATHENE *(brightly)* Hallo. *(She beams at him)*

VERNON Who are you? *(He eyes the cleaver, nervously)*

ATHENE *(reasonably)* Aunt Athene, dear. *(Prompting)* One of the Family.

VERNON *(blankly)* Family?

ATHENE The *Tomb* family.

VERNON *(waspishly)* I don't know about Tomb Family. From where *I'm* standing you look more like one of the *Addams* family. *(He relaxes slightly)* Gordon Bennett. I thought you were going to do a Sweeney Todd number on me. *(He fingers his throat)*

ATHENE *(simpering)* Don't be silly, dear. I wouldn't kill *you*. You're one of *us*, aren't you?

VERNON No. I'm *not*. I'm one of *them*. *(Quickly)* The others, I mean. The helpers. With the housework. *(He remembers his manners)* Prewitt's the name. *Vernon* Prewitt. *(He extends a limp hand)* Professional actor and part-time domestic ancillary.

ATHENE *(disappointed)* Oh. But I thought you were someone else. A relation of ours from Gravesend.

VERNON *(doubtfully)* Well... I have *had* relations in Gravesend— *(coyly)* but I'm not saying who with. *(He smirks)*

ATHENE *(frowning)* Then if you're not one of the family, what were you doing in cousin Dora's chair? *(She indicates it with the cleaver)*

VERNON *(recoiling again)* Nothing. I was having a rest.

ATHENE *(annoyed)* But you haven't any right. It was Dora's *favourite*. She hardly ever sat anywhere else. *(Primly)* The *police* said she was sitting there the night she died. *(Serenely)* It must have been *such* a comfort during her last seconds. *(She gazes at the chair fondly)*

VERNON *(startled)* You mean... *(He looks askance at the chair)*

ATHENE *(matter-of-factly)* Oh, yes. She was strangled, you see. With her very own evening scarf. Black moiré chiffon with real jet bugle bead fringing.

VERNON *(aghast)* How awful.

ATHENE I know. She should never have worn black with her colouring. It didn't suit her at all. *(Suddenly brandishing the cleaver again)* So this isn't yours, then? I found it in the passages and the blood's quite fresh—

VERNON *(moving back)* No. No. I—I—I've never seen it before.

ATHENE *(looking at the cleaver in a puzzled manner)* Then I wonder what it was doing there? None of the family would use it. Not for business, anyway. It's far too old-fashioned. *(Proudly)* We've always preferred sophisticated methods, you see. Thallium and Hyoscine, for instance... *(She remembers)* though we have experimented with Ricin a few times. And CCNU. *(She shrugs)* Still—if it isn't yours, I'd better take it to the kitchen before someone has an accident.

VERNON *(uncomfortably)* I think *I've* already had one.

AUGUSTUS *enters.*

AUGUSTUS *(pompously)* Ah, there you are, Athene. I've been looking all over... *(He sees* VERNON*)* And who is *this*, might I ask?

ATHENE Mr Prewitt, dear. One of Mr Crayle's people. *(To* VERNON*)* My brother Augustus. *(She whispers)* He's a *doctor.*

VERNON Oh? *(He flashes a smile)* Hallo. *(He holds out his hand)*

AUGUSTUS *(ignoring him)* I am most displeased, Athene. Most displeased.

ATHENE *(anxiously)* What is it, Augustus? What's happened?

AUGUSTUS *(grandly)* When I go to the bathroom to perform my ablutions, I do not expect to find half-naked young men inside it.

VERNON *(wide-eyed)* Neither do I, but I live in hope.

AUGUSTUS *(glancing at him in irritation)* What is *more*...he was removing his...his...*cosmetics* with *my* face-cloth.

VERNON *(easily)* Ooh, I wouldn't worry about that, love. You should see what some of the queens *I know take theirs* off with. *(He winces)* It's enough to turn your stomach.

AUGUSTUS *(fiercely)* Will you be *quiet.*

VERNON *recoils.*

(to ATHENE*)* Who is he? That's what I want to know. Who *is* he?

LARRY *limps hastily into the room. He has removed his make-up, hat, wig and frilled collar, and his costume is unbuttoned.*

LARRY *(breathlessly)* Oh, there you are. Look. I'm terribly sorry. I'd no idea. There isn't a washbasin in my room, you see, and...

AUGUSTUS *(turning to him, furiously)* Your room? *Your* room? *All* rooms in *this* house are *my* rooms.

ATHENE *(interrupting) Our* rooms, Augustus. The Family's.

AUGUSTUS *(sharply)* As the only male, I speak for everyone, Athene. Now please be silent. I will not have strangers parading around the house without *my* express permission.

LARRY If you'll let me explain...

AUGUSTUS There is no need for explanation. You will leave Monument House at once. Do you understand? At once. *(He glares at him)*

LARRY *(tightly)* There's nothing I'd like better, but I *can't.* I had an accident at the bottom of the drive and my van's wrapped round the gatepost. I can't go anywhere till I get some help.

ATHENE *(concerned)* But you can't stay *here.* Not in *this* house.

LARRY It's not through choice, believe me. But Miss Fabia said...

AUGUSTUS *(sharply)* Fabia? You know cousin Fabia?

LARRY Well...we met about half an hour ago.

AUGUSTUS *(fuming)* I might have known it. Not in the house five minutes and already undermining my authority. I won't have it, Athene. Do you hear me? I won't *have* it.

AUGUSTUS *storms out.*

LARRY *(looking after him in amazement)* Bit excitable, isn't he?

ATHENE *(uncomfortably)* He's not been himself, today. Not since lunchtime. He must have eaten something that disagreed with him.

VERNON It wouldn't dare.

LARRY *(to* **ATHENE***)* Look. If it's going to cause problems, I'll try and make it to the village.

VERNON And what about me? What am I supposed to do? I've got the room next to his. *(He indicates* **LARRY***)*

ATHENE *(biting her lip)* Oh, dear. It's very difficult. If Fabia said you could stay...

LARRY She *did*.

VERNON *(quickly)* She did.

ATHENE *(reluctantly)* Then I suppose you'd better. But it's *very* confusing. She knows the rules as well as *we* do.

LARRY You don't have to worry, Miss—er—

ATHENE Tomb.

LARRY Miss Tomb. I'll keep well out of the way, and as soon as it's daylight, I'll be out of your hair for good.

VERNON And me. I never have been a country girl. Give me the bright lights, any time.

ATHENE *(concerned)* Oh, I *wish* I knew what was happening.

ATHENE *exits.*

VERNON She's not the only one. If the rest of 'em are anything like the ones *I've* met, they're *all* a few sandwiches short of a picnic.

LARRY *(agreeing)* They do seem a bit peculiar, don't they? *(He sits on the* chaise*)* If I thought I could make it on this leg, I'd try to find a place in the village. *(He presses it gently and grimaces)* I wonder if they'd mind me having a bath? Some hot water might help it.

VERNON You'd better make it quick. They'll be having dinner in a few minutes.

LARRY I'm not that hungry, to be honest. I filled up on jelly and sausage rolls. Besides...this is all the gear I've got. My real clothes are back in the van. *(Miserably)* God, What a mess.

VERNON *(diffidently)* Have you—er—been in show business long?

LARRY *(tiredly)* Not really. A few years. Why?

VERNON *(coyly)* Well... I've just turned pro, myself... *(Hastily)* But I'm not a beginner. I've been with the amateurs for years. *(Proudly)* LAMDA Gold Medal and Distinction and three Merits at the Basildon Festival. But I knew it was time to move on. Especially after last year's *Midsummer Night's Dream*. Everybody *raved* about my Bottom.

LARRY *(smiling wanly)* I'm sure you'll make a better go of it than I did. The last time *I* played Shakesp... *(He stops short and turns to look over his shoulder)* What was that?

VERNON *(frowning)* What was what?

LARRY That...*noise*. It seemed to come from behind that bookcase. *(He gets up and limps towards the secret door)*

VERNON *(distastefully)* Probably rats. The place is swarming with 'em. Half the size of cows if the traps in the cellars are anything to go by.

LARRY *(standing by the bookcase)* Can't hear anything now. *(He turns and surveys the room curiously)* Wonder what happened to the books.

VERNON *(shrugging)* No use asking me, dear. I never set eyes on the place till this morning.

LARRY *(wearily)* Well... I'd better be off for that bath. I—er—I'll see you tomorrow perhaps?

LARRY *moves painfully towards the door and exits.*

VERNON *(following to the doorway)* I'll tell 'em you won't be down for dinner, then. *(He calls)* But if you feel peckish during the night, just knock on the wall and I'll be right in. I never go to bed without a few munchies, so I'm sure to have *something* you can nibble on.

LARRY *(offstage)* I'll try to remember that.

VERNON *(moving back into the room)* Ooh, he'll go far, will that one. Oooh, I think there's just time for a little libation before dinner. *(He crosses to the drinks table and studies it)* Now then—what is it my old Granny likes to say? Gin makes you grin... Sherry makes you merry... Whisky makes you frisky... *(He picks up a decanter)* So *I'd* better settle for *brandy.*

EDNA *(offstage)* Vernon? Are you there, Vernon?

He turns towards the doors as EDNA *hurries in, followed by a fuming* ZOE.

(breathlessly) Oh, Vernon. It's Mr Crayle. We can't find him anywhere. We've looked all over the house but there isn't a sign.

VERNON *(drily)* Oooh, I'm crying my eyes out. *(Reassuringly)* Don't worry, darlin'. Just lift the nearest rock, and I'm sure you'll find him under it. *(He pours a drink)*

ZOE *(sharply)* This is *serious*, Mr Prewitt. He isn't here.

VERNON *(exasperated)* Well what do you want *me* to do about it? I mean—he can't have gone far, can he? There's nowhere to go to. *(He thinks)* Unless he's outside. You know? Gone for a walk.

ZOE *(scornfully)* In thick *fog*?

VERNON Don't knock it, darlin'. Some of my best walks have been done in thick fog. *(He replaces the decanter on the table, picks up his glass and moves to her)* He's probably gone down the drive to have a look at the damage. We all know what *solicitors* are like. If there's a chance of making a few quid out of somebody else's problems, they're like wasps round a jam-pot.

ZOE *(indignantly)* I beg your pardon?

VERNON *(darkly)* I bet he's going to sue that poor cow upstairs for scratching the gatepost.

EDNA *(hopefully)* You wouldn't go and look, would you? Just in case he's got lost.

VERNON *(incredulously)* What do you think *I* am? A Saint Bernard? I'm not trolling all the way down there. Let him find his own way back.

EDNA But dinner's ready and we can't start without *him*. *(Despairingly)* It'll be ruined if he doesn't come soon. *(She pleads)* Please, Vernon.

VERNON *(with ill grace)* Oh, all right, then. But if I come down with bubonic plague from tramping about in that lot, I shall hold you personally responsible. *(He hands her his glass)* Look after this while I get my coat.

VERNON *exits huffily.*

EDNA *(calling after him)* Thanks, Vernon. I'll make it up to you.

ZOE I'll check his room again.

ZOE *exits quickly.*

EDNA *looks at the glass in her hand, undecided what to do with it. She finally moves to the drinks table and picks up the decanter* VERNON *used.*

She is about to pour the brandy back into it, when HENRIETTA *enters.*

HENRIETTA *(acidly)* Who was that just left? Octavia's nancy-boy?

EDNA *(turning to her; startled)* Oh, you didn't half make me jump, miss. I didn't hear you coming.

HENRIETTA So I see. *(Pointedly)* Do you always help yourself to other people's drinks? *(She moves towards her)*

EDNA *(protesting)* I wasn't, miss. I was pouring it back. It hasn't been touched, you see, and it seemed such a shame to waste it.

HENRIETTA *(drily)* Really? What a thrifty little soul you are. In that case, you'd better leave it with *me*. I'm sure *I* can find a use for it. *(She takes the glass from* **EDNA** *and moves up to the fireplace)* So where did they find *you*, then? The local cats' home? *(She takes a drink)*

EDNA *(uncertainly)* Dengie Road, miss. In Haslow.

HENRIETTA Haslow? *(Heavily)* I presume by *that* you mean *Hag's Hollow*?

EDNA Well...yes, miss. But everybody calls it Haslow. *(As an afterthought)* Except for tourists...and strangers.

HENRIETTA *(coldly)* Really? Well for your information, it's been Hag's Hollow for the last five hundred years, and that's what *this* family *still* calls it. *(Firmly)* Hag's Hollow. *(She sips again)*

EDNA *(uncomfortably)* I suppose somebody thought Haslow sounded *nicer.* You know. More... *(She struggles for the word)* politically correct and things. I mean...people see Hag's Hollow on the signposts and they think it's a joke. They're always asking Mrs Harris in the café if she brews her tea in a cauldron.

HENRIETTA *(moving downstage left)* And speaking of cauldrons, what time do *we* eat tonight? Assuming of course, we *shall* be eating.

EDNA *(quickly putting the decanter down)* It's all ready *now*, miss. I can serve it as soon as Mr Crayle gets back.

HENRIETTA *(turning to look at her)* Back?

EDNA From wherever it is he went, miss.

HENRIETTA You mean...he's not in the house?

EDNA *(uneasily)* No, miss. We can't find him anywhere. That's why Vernon's gone *outside*. To see if he's there.

HENRIETTA *looks at the window.*

HENRIETTA He wouldn't see him in that lot if he *fell* on him. *(Curiously)* How long's he been missing?

EDNA I'm not sure, miss. About twenty minutes, I think.

HENRIETTA And what about his fancy piece? The secretary. Doesn't *she* know where he is?

EDNA No, miss. And she seems ever so cross about it. She's just gone upstairs to check his room again.

HENRIETTA'*s eyes narrow and she sinks into thought.*

OCTAVIA *enters the room.*

OCTAVIA *(firmly)* Henrietta. We have to talk.

HENRIETTA *(without turning)* Later.

OCTAVIA Now. *(She grasps* HENRIETTA'*s arm and pulls her round)* Listen to me. *(She releases her)* I have just received a warning. *(With great emphasis)* From *cousin Marcus.*

HENRIETTA *(amused)* You're even battier than I thought you were. He's been dead for months. *(She begins to turn away)*

EDNA *looks at* OCTAVIA *wide-eyed.*

OCTAVIA *(grasping* HENRIETTA'*s arm again)* Death is no barrier to communication. *(Insistently)* He came to warn us, Henrietta. Someone here is in *grave danger.*

HENRIETTA *(acidly)* Yes. Of getting her bony fingers broken if she doesn't let go my arm.

OCTAVIA *(hastily releasing her)* We have to warn the others. Before it's too late. He was most insistent.

HENRIETTA Was he now? And what exactly did he have to say for himself? Beware the Ides of March?

OCTAVIA *(in dramatic tones)* "She dreamt tonight she saw my statue, which, like a fountain with a hundred spouts, did run pure blood; and many lusty Romans came smiling, and did bathe their hands in it."

HENRIETTA *(sourly)* And what's *that* supposed to mean?

EDNA *(helpfully)* It's from Shakespeare, miss. *Julius Caesar.*

HENRIETTA and **OCTAVIA** *turn and look at her.*

(cowed) We did it at school.

FABIA *enters breezily.*

FABIA Didn't we all, darlin'? Didn't we all? And I remember the *fun* we had *doing* it. *(She cackles coarsely)* Evenin' Tavie... Henrietta. Both keepin' well, I see. *(She totters to the wing chair; to EDNA)* Get me a sherry, darlin'. Always like a drinky-poos before dinner. *(She sits heavily)*

EDNA *begins to search for the sherry.*

(to the others) So how's tricks, then? Still getting plenty?

OCTAVIA *(tightly)* Nothing has changed, I see. As coarse as ever you were.

HENRIETTA *(pointedly)* But much older. And twice as fat.

FABIA *(cheerily)* You're right about that, Hetty. But at least I don't have to *shave* twice a day like *some* folk I could mention.

HENRIETTA *glowers as* **EDNA** *scurries round to* **FABIA** *with the sherry.*

(taking the glass) Thanks, darlin'. *(To the others)* Cheers. *(She takes a sip)* So what's all this about Crayle being missing?

OCTAVIA *(blankly)* Crayle? *(She glances at* **HENRIETTA***)*

HENRIETTA According to her, *(she indicates* **EDNA** *with her head)* he seems to have gone walkabout.

FABIA *(easily)* Well, he can't have gone far. I was talking to him meself only half an hour ago.

HENRIETTA The point is, why should he have gone *anywhere*? If you ask me, I think we should have a chat with little Miss

Efficiency, upstairs. There's something going on here I'm not too happy about.

OCTAVIA Henrietta's right. And after Marcus's warning tonight...

FABIA *(amused)* Oh, my gawd. You're not still on *that* kick, are you? Ghosties and Ghoulies and things that go bonk in the night. *(Scornfully)* It's all mumbo jumbo, darlin', and them who says otherwise want their bumps feeling. *(She finishes her drink)* Give us another one, sweetheart. *(She holds up the glass)*

EDNA *scuttles down to refill it.*

OCTAVIA *(icily)* For your information, Fabia, there's nothing of the mumbo jumbo in communicating with the dead, and I can quote you the highest authority on *that* matter. The Holy *Bible*. Samuel. Chapter twenty-eight. King Saul and the Witch of Endor.

A worried-looking **ATHENE** *enters.*

FABIA And speaking of witches... *(To* **ATHENE***)* Hallo, Athene.

ATHENE *(distractedly)* Hallo, dear. Has anyone seen... *(She sees* **EDNA***)* Oh, there you are, dear. I don't want to worry you, but there seems to be something burning in the kitchen.

EDNA *(sniffing the air quickly and wailing)* The cabbage.

EDNA *thrusts the decanter into* **OCTAVIA***'s hands and dashes out of the room.*

ATHENE *(calling after her)* I've left the cleaver on the draining board.

She turns to see everyone looking at her.

(defensively) Well, I had to wash it. It was covered in blood.

HENRIETTA *(after a moment)* Blood?

ATHENE It was all over the blade. I can't think *who'd* have used it...*or* who they'd use it on. *(She shudders)* Such a *common* instrument.

FABIA And where exactly did you find it, darlin'? Can you remember?

ATHENE *(indignantly)* Well, of course I can. I'm not *entirely* senile. It was in the passageway. Behind there. *(She indicates the bookcase)*

HENRIETTA *(firmly)* Crayle. It has to be Crayle.

OCTAVIA *(triumphantly)* I *knew* it. The spirits are never wrong. *(She puts the decanter on the table and sits on the chaise, smugly)*

ATHENE *(puzzled)* I don't understand. What about him?

HENRIETTA *(scornfully)* He's the one who got the chop, you birdbrain. That's why they couldn't find him. Somebody's given that ratty little hairpiece of his a new parting and dumped him in the marshes.

ATHENE *(shocked)* You mean...he's *dead*?

FABIA *(easily)* It's a reasonable guess, darlin'. The question is, though...who did it? And *why*?

OCTAVIA *(defensively)* Well, obviously it wasn't one of *us*. We'd hardly dispose of him before we found out why he'd brought us all here. *(Firmly)* It *has* to be one of the outsiders.

HENRIETTA And how'd they know about the passageways?

OCTAVIA What does *that* matter? *(She twists her lips)* Dispose of them *now*, is what *I* say. Better to be safe than sorry.

FABIA She *has* got a point, Hetty. I mean...we'll *have* to get rid of 'em before we leave here, won't we? Can't have loose ends lying around. *(She frowns)* All the same... I'd like to know *why* he was killed. If there's one thing I *can't* stand, it's bleedin' mysteries.

HENRIETTA *(glancing into the hall)* Well, here comes somebody who might have some answers for us.

ZOE *enters, with a fixed smile on her face.*

ZOE *(graciously)* I'm terribly sorry to keep you all waiting. The fact is...we seem to have lost Mr Crayle. I can't *think* where he's hiding himself. *(She laughs falsely)*

FABIA *(easily)* Oh, I shouldn't worry about it, dear. I think *we* might be able to come up with a few suggestions.

OCTAVIA But whilst we're *waiting,* perhaps you'd like to tell us exactly what we're doing here? *(She fixes ZOE with a basilisk-like stare)*

ZOE Well... I'm sure Mr Crayle would prefer to tell you himself.

HENRIETTA *(coldly)* No doubt he would. But as he isn't here and you *are*...

FABIA *(with a chilling smile)* And we've always been rather impatient as a family...

ATHENE We'll let you put us out of our misery. *(She beams)*

ZOE *(tightly)* There's nothing I'd like better. *(She forces a smile)* Well, there's no great *secret* about it...

HENRIETTA Good.

FABIA We never have liked secrets. *(To the others)* Have we, girls?

The others shake their heads.

ZOE *(indicating the drinks table)* Would anyone like a drink?

FABIA *raises her glass and shakes it slightly.* HENRIETTA *indicates the glass she holds.* OCTAVIA *does not react at all, and* ATHENE *shakes her head.* ZOE *stares at the glasses and then at the drinks table before relaxing.*

Well...as you already know. With the deaths of your cousins and the other named legatees of your late uncle's will...under the rules of Intestacy, it would appear that this house and its contents should be equally divided between yourselves.

HENRIETTA *(sharply)* Appear? What do you mean...*appear?* Of course it comes to us. There's no question about it.

ZOE *(sweetly)* Unfortunately there *is*, Miss Tomb. You see Miss Monica's body was never found, so her death can only be *assumed*. At the present moment, in the eyes of the law, the entire estate is *hers*. It may be several years before she's legally declared dead.

OCTAVIA *(in disbelief)* Years?

ZOE I'm afraid so. *(She smiles sweetly)*

FABIA So what are we doing here, then?

ZOE Let me get you another drink. *(She crosses to the drinks table and picks up a decanter)* Mr Crayle had a thought. Not entirely *ethical*, you understand... *(She smiles winningly)* but a perfectly legal loop-hole that would perhaps allow you to claim your inheritance much sooner than expected. *(She fills two glasses)* He thought you should get what you deserved as quickly as possible.

HENRIETTA And what *is* this "perfectly legal loophole"?

ZOE *(quickly)* Oh, I've no idea. I'm only his secretary, you see. But I *do* know he wanted to explain it to you face to face, and that's why he asked you to come. *(Gushing)* He's such a brilliant man. I'm sure you're in for a really unexpected surprise. *(She crosses to ATHENE and thrusts a glass into her hand before turning to OCTAVIA)*

FABIA *(to herself)* We're not the only ones, darlin'.

ZOE *(extending the glass to OCTAVIA and looking at FABIA)* I'm sorry?

FABIA Just thinking aloud.

OCTAVIA *(flatly)* I don't drink, thank you.

ZOE *(pressing)* But surely a little toast to your *forthcoming prosperity* can't do any harm?

OCTAVIA *(glowering)* I told you. I don't dr—

ZOE *suddenly lets out a startled gasp and the glass drops from her hand.*

ATHENE *(startled)* What is it?

ZOE *(staring at the french windows)* There's someone out there. In the shrubbery.

OCTAVIA *and* FABIA *struggle to their feet as* HENRIETTA *pushes her glass at* ATHENE *and rapidly crosses to the windows to wrestle with the handles.*

ATHENE *(calling anxiously)* Be careful.

HENRIETTA *flings open the windows and exits.*

HENRIETTA *(offstage; fiercely)* Right. Let's have a look at you.

With a cry, LARRY *is flung through the windows and into the room. His hair is wet and he is naked but for a large, grubby, bath towel wrapped around his waist, which he clutches tightly. Everyone stares at him.*

ZOE *(surprised)* Mr Lewiss.

FABIA Well... I know I fancied seeing more of him, but I didn't expect it to be *this* soon.

HENRIETTA *enters.*

LARRY *(babbling)* I'm sorry. I'm sorry. I mean...it isn't what it looks like. I was just...just... I... *(Despairingly)* Oh, God.

ZOE *(icily)* And *what* do you think you're playing at, if you don't mind my asking? Are you some sort of *pervert*?

LARRY *(taken aback)* No. Of course not.

HENRIETTA Then perhaps you wouldn't mind explaining what you were doing outside with nothing but a towel wrapped round you?

FABIA *(drinking in his physique)* Well, whatever it was, he must have been doing it *beautifully.*

ATHENE *(reprovingly)* Fabia. *(She deposits the glasses on the library table)*

OCTAVIA re-seats herself and fixes **LARRY** with a baleful gaze.

LARRY *(hastily)* It was an accident. I mean... I didn't know where I was. It all happened so fast.

ZOE Oh?

OCTAVIA *(extracting one of her "pins")* I think you should tell us everything, Mr Lewiss. *(She runs her thumb gently over the point)* Just to clear up any...misunderstandings.

LARRY Yes. Yes. Of course. *(He glances round at them all)* Well... It all started when I went upstairs. To have a bath. I was just washing my hair when I heard the door opening... though I could have sworn I'd locked it... but I couldn't see a thing with the soap in my eyes, and by the time I'd washed it away...the lights'd gone out. I knew there was somebody in there with me, but they didn't answer when I shouted. It was quite scary. I was just getting out of the water, when whoever it was did a runner and slammed the door behind them. By the time I'd grabbed a towel and found the light switch, they were long gone.

ATHENE *(impressed)* And you've no idea who it was?

LARRY *(shaking his head)* Not a clue.

HENRIETTA So how did you end up out there? *(She indicates)*

LARRY I couldn't open the door. The knob had dropped off when it slammed, and the other half must have been somewhere outside. And that's when I noticed my clothes had gone.

ZOE *(frowning)* Clothes?

LARRY The clown suit and things. Whoever had been in there, had pinched the lot.

FABIA *(suggestively)* I can think of a few things *I'd* like to pinch, darlin', but they wouldn't include a *clown costume*. *(Puzzled)* What they want that for?

LARRY I haven't a clue. But there I was, stuck in the bathroom with nothing but a towel to wrap round me...and that's when I thought of the window. I was hoping there'd be a drainpipe or something I could climb down, but I couldn't get *that* open either. I was tugging on the catch when it snapped off in my hand and I went flying backwards into the wall. And that's where the *weird* bit comes in. One minute I was in the bathroom, and the next I was in some sort of corridor. It was pitch black, but I felt my way along it till I came out into bushes at the side of the house. I couldn't believe it. I was just trying to work out where I was when I spotted the light in here *(To* HENRIETTA*)* and *you* came charging out and grabbed me.

HENRIETTA *(flatly)* P'raps it's a good job I did. They can be quite dangerous, gardens can. Especially the ones round *this* place.

ATHENE We're right on the edge of the marsh, you see. Another few minutes and we might never have seen you again.

FABIA And I can't tell you how much *that'd* have upset us. *(To* HENRIETTA*)* Shut the windows, Hettie. Poor feller's coming out in goose bumps.

LARRY *(shivering)* It *is* a bit chilly.

HENRIETTA *closes the windows.*

FABIA *(putting her arm around* LARRY*'s shoulders)* Don't worry, darlin'. I've got one or two ideas for warming you up again. But in the meantime, we'd better find you something to wear. *(To* ZOE*)* I'm sure the boys had a few bits that'll fit him.

ZOE *(coldly)* We've put all the clothing to one side. *(To* LARRY, *balefully)* If you follow me, I'll show you where it is.

ZOE *turns and walks out of the room.*

LARRY *(to* FABIA*)* Thanks.

LARRY *quickly limps after* ZOE.

There is a momentary silence.

OCTAVIA Interesting. *(She replaces the "pin" in her hair)*

HENRIETTA What is? *(She moves towards the fireplace)*

ATHENE That *story* he told us. Fancy him finding the bathroom passageway. I'd even forgotten *that* one myself.

FABIA And who'd want a tatty old clown costume? *(She sits)* Not one of us. Besides...we were all in here.

ATHENE Except for Augustus... *(Thoughtfully)* and Mr Prewitt, of course.

HENRIETTA You needn't worry about *him.* He's outside, somewhere. Searching for Crayle.

FABIA *(puzzled)* So it *must* have been Gussie.

ATHENE *(pained)* I wish you wouldn't call him that, Fabia. You know he doesn't like it. And why would Augustus want a clown suit?

FABIA It'd be an improvement on the stuff he usually wears.

ATHENE *gives her a disapproving look.*

OCTAVIA *(harshly)* You're all missing the point. *(She rises)* It doesn't matter *who* took the clown suit. Or why. What *does* matter is that that woman knows more than she's letting on. Didn't any of you spot it?

HENRIETTA What?

OCTAVIA *(contemptuously)* When he mentioned the *tunnels,* she never batted an eyelid.

ATHENE Why should she? We all *know* about them.

OCTAVIA *(pointedly)* Yes. But she *shouldn't*. She's an outsider. The tunnels are *a family* secret. She has no right to even know they exist.

HENRIETTA So...

FABIA Just a minute. Just a minute. I can't think straight. You mean   she's the one who finished Crayle off? But why?

OCTAVIA I don't know. But I intend to find out.

FABIA *(putting a hand to her head)* Gawd. My head's thumping. Has anybody got an aspirin?

ATHENE *(helpfully)* There's probably something in the sick-room. Would you like me to look?

FABIA *(waving it aside)* No. No. I'll be all right. Lack of food, I expect.

HENRIETTA *(sourly)* You can certainly say that again. Are we ever going to get anything to eat in this place? I'm starting to get the gripes, myself.

FABIA *(struggling to her feet)* Let's go find out what's happening. I'm going to be good for nothing, if I don't get a bit of sustenance.

She staggers and ATHENE *hastily supports her.*

Whoops-a-daisy. Getting a bit tottery in me old age. *(She cackles)* Steady as she goes, darlin'.

With ATHENE *supporting* FABIA, *they exit into the hall and vanish from sight.*

HENRIETTA *(to* OCTAVIA*)* Coming? *(She begins to follow the others)*

OCTAVIA *(primly)* I think I'll stay here a while. There's someone on the other side trying to make contact with me. Someone important. I can feel the vibrations.

HENRIETTA *(drily)* Knowing this place, sweetie, it's more likely to be *subsidence.*

HENRIETTA *exits.*

Throwing a look of disgust at **HENRIETTA**'s *departing figure,* **OCTAVIA** *moves to the wing chair, sits, leans back and closes her eyes.*

OCTAVIA *(softly)* I am here. Waiting for you. Come. Draw closer. Closer. Tell me your purpose.

A scowling **ZOE** *enters the room and stops short on seeing* **OCTAVIA.**

(her voice assuming sepulchral tones) Speak to me. Reveal your secrets. Louder. Louder. I cannot hear you. Ah, yes. Yes. I understand. You are lost. Lost in the house of blood.

ZOE *takes a step back as though to exit, then catches sight of the paper knife on the writing desk.*

A warning. You give me a warning?

ZOE *looks into the hall and seeing no-one, swiftly snatches up the paper knife. Clutching it tightly, she creeps down behind* **OCTAVIA**, *preparing to stab.*

Beware the hands of strangers. Beware the hands of those who claim to befriend you. *(In normal tones and without opening her eyes)* I wouldn't *do* that, if I were you, Mrs Mapleton. I really wouldn't. *(She opens her eyes and sits up)*

ZOE *stands there in shock.*

You didn't *actually* think you stood a chance of killing me, did you? *(She rises)* If you did, then it shows how little you know about the Tombs. *(Grandly)* We were professional killers before *your* unfortunate ancestors descended from their rather pathetic family trees. *(She removes a "pin" from her hairpiece)* So you see, my dear...you never had a chance from the word "Go". *(She moves towards her, the "pin" pointed at* ZOE's *throat)* Now let us find out *exactly* what is going on in Monument House, shall we?

The secret panel begins to open and the Clown's figure steps into the room. Instead of the usual face, however, it wears a hideous Halloween mask. One hand is behind its back.

(glancing at the Clown) Ah. Just in time, Augustus. Mrs Mapleton is about to tell us a bedtime story. *(She presses the "pin" to* ZOE's *throat) Do* make a start.

As the knife drops from ZOE's *nerveless fingers, the Clown's hand comes from behind its back. It is holding a gun.*

(surprised) What are you doing, Augustus? There's no need for...

The Clown points the gun at OCTAVIA *and fires.* OCTAVIA *stiffens, then turns up stage to collapse.* ZOE *looks at the Clown in amazement. The Clown gives a deep bow, tosses the gun to her, which she involuntarily catches.*

The Clown steps back into the opening and vanishes.

The panel closes. Stunned, ZOE *looks at the body of* OCTAVIA *and then at the gun in her hand.*

FABIA *appears in the doorway and regards the scene.*

FABIA *(amused)* Oh, dear, dear. Looks like somebody *has* been naughty.

ZOE *turns to face her as—.*

—the curtains fall.

ACT II

Scene One

The same. Half an hour later.

OCTAVIA's body has been removed, and the knife replaced on the desk, but otherwise the room is as before.

HENRIETTA sits at the library table, munching at a "doorstop" sandwich and clutching a large glass of milk. A dinner plate, piled high with more sandwiches, is on the downstage edge of the table. ZOE sits apparently brokenly on the chaise, a handkerchief crushed in her hand, mopping at her eyes. An uncomfortable LARRY in ill-fitting clothing of tasteless colours and wearing slippers, sits with one arm around her shoulders, comforting her, whilst FABIA stands behind them and to one side, holding the gun loosely. ATHENE, concentrating hard, stoops over the open Bible, writing carefully on the flyleaf with a large quill pen. An inkwell from the desk is on the table beside her. AUGUSTUS, a fierce scowl on his face, is standing with his back to the fire, holding a glass of whisky.

FABIA *(easily)* So let's go through it again, darlin'. Just to keep things straight. You took Mr Lewiss upstairs to get him some clothes, left him to try things on, then came straight back down here again to check on the dinner?

ZOE glances up and nods miserably.

After helping put the fire out, you...

AUGUSTUS *(sharply)* Fire? Fire? *What* Fire?

HENRIETTA *(grunting)* Nothing to get excited about. Girl put everything under the grill to keep warm while she scraped out the cabbage pan, and the whole lot went up in flames. Silly cow tried to put it out with the soup. That's why we're eating these. *(She brandishes the sandwich)*

FABIA *(tartly)* You mean that's why *you* are. The rest of us haven't had a look in, yet.

HENRIETTA And whose fault's that? They've been sitting there for the past five minutes. Besides...I'm hungry. *(She takes another bite and washes it down with milk)*

ATHENE *(satisfied)* There. *(She reads brightly)* Octavia Tomb, born nineteen thirty-two, assassinated nineteen ninety-eight. *(She beams happily)*

LARRY *(looking up with a pained expression)* It's a bit—*stark*, isn't it?

ATHENE *(frowning at him)* Stark?

LARRY For a family bible.

ATHENE *(reasonably)* But how else can we keep records, Mr Lewiss? We're a very old family. There are *hundreds* of names in this book and we have to keep them in order.

LARRY Well, yes. I suppose so. But...*assassinated*?

ATHENE *(realizing)* Oh, I see. Yes. Yes. But we *always* enter the cause of death. *(She turns back to the book and reads)* Julia Tomb... Nineteen twenty-one... Poisoned with salts of lemon. *(Confidentially)* Old-fashioned, but very effective. *(She reads again)* Vespasian Tomb. Nineteen forty-five... Beheaded in car crash. Caligula Tomb... Octavia's father... Nineteen fifty-three... Hiccups.

LARRY *(surprised)* Hiccups?

ATHENE *(uncomfortable)* Well...not the hiccups *themselves*... more the *cure*, I'm afraid. Someone suggested we gave him a shock...so Augustus wired his bath-taps to the overhead power lines. It fried him to a crisp when he turned them on.

HENRIETTA *(looking up)* And blacked out half of Cheltenham.

ATHENE *(hurt)* Poor Augustus. It was only a childish prank, but Octavia *never* really forgave him.

FABIA *(tartly)* If nobody minds, I'd like to get back to what's happened here *tonight*. *(She glares at* ATHENE, *then turns back to* ZOE) So you helped put the fire out, slipped into the loo to tidy yourself up again, then started back here to tell *us* what had happened? Right?

ZOE *(nodding)* But just as I got to the door, I heard voices. Angry voices. Threatening. I looked inside and there they were. The man in the clown suit and Octavia. She said "You won't get away with this, Augustus. The Family won't stand for it"... Then he pointed the gun at her and fired. *(She breaks down, sobbing)* It was horrible. Horrible.

LARRY *comforts her.*

AUGUSTUS *(snorting)* Ridiculous. Absolutely ridiculous. *(He takes a drink)*

FABIA *(ignoring him)* And then what happened?

ZOE *(mopping at her eyes)* He turned and saw me, threw the gun, and went though a door behind that bookcase. *(She indicates it and sobs loudly)*

LARRY *(holding her)* Look. Can't we leave it now? You can see how upset she is. Somebody's *got* to go for the police.

HENRIETTA You volunteering? *(She swills some more milk)*

LARRY *(stung)* If you like. We can't just *sit* here. Besides...it was *my* outfit he was wearing.

FABIA Who was?

LARRY *(indicating* AUGUSTUS) Him.

AUGUSTUS *glowers at him.*

You heard what she said. Octavia called him Augustus.

ATHENE *(protesting)* But it *couldn't* have been Augustus. He was looking through Lucien's things in the old laboratory.

LARRY *(disbelievingly)* So he says.

AUGUSTUS *(fiercely)* I am not accustomed to people doubting my word.

FABIA *(easily)* Course not, darlin'. But the fact is, you and Tavie ~~weren't exactly the best of pals, were you? And with her out~~ of the way, you get a bit bigger share of what's on offer, if you get my meaning.

AUGUSTUS *(outraged)* This is monstrous. I absolutely refuse to listen to this vile accusation. *(He stalks to the library table and slams down his glass)*

HENRIETTA *(easily)* Keep your shirt on, Gussie. We all know you wouldn't have the guts to face Octavia on your own. Even in a clown suit. *(Thoughtfully)* But there's somebody else who might. *(With great deliberation)* Little Miss Nancy-boy.

LARRY *(blankly)* Who? *(He realizes)* You mean... *Vernon?*

HENRIETTA Why not? Just because he's a poofter it doesn't mean he couldn't handle a gun...or swing a nifty little meat cleaver.

ZOE *(puzzled)* What's a meat cleaver got to do with it?

HENRIETTA That's what he used on Crayle. *(She gulps on her milk)*

There is a startled reaction from ZOE, LARRY *and* AUGUSTUS.

AUGUSTUS *(spluttering)* You mean *he's* dead, too?

FABIA As a doornail, darlin'. That's why they couldn't find him. He's probably down the bottom of the marsh by this time.

LARRY *(dazed)* But... But *why?* I mean...it doesn't make *sense.* He told me himself he'd never met Crayle until today.

FABIA Best not to believe *everything* somebody tells you, darlin'. There's some very devious people around these days.

LARRY (*protesting*) But nobody goes round killing perfect strangers.

ATHENE (*indignantly*) We do.

LARRY (*throwing a startled glance at her*) But there's got to be a *reason*.

FABIA Maybe there is, but it doesn't look like we're going to find out what it was. Not at the moment, anyway. Perhaps Hettie's right. Prewitt *did* bump 'em off, and now he's done a runner.

HENRIETTA 'Course I'm right. We'll not see him again.

VERNON enters in his outdoor clothing.

VERNON (*peevishly*) Well, he's not out *there*. I've been right down the bottom of the flaming drive.

Everyone stares at him.

(*startled*) What? (*He looks from one to the other*) What?

LARRY (*standing*) What have you done with my clown suit?

ZOE (*savagely*) You'll get thirty years for this, you—you—

ATHENE (*hissing*) Murderer. (*She glares at him*)

VERNON gapes at them all.

VERNON What are you talking about?

AUGUSTUS (*glowering*) Don't play the innocent with *us*. *We* know you did it.

VERNON What? *What?*

LARRY (*flatly*) Somebody killed Octavia. About quarter of an hour ago.

VERNON (*looking for the missing face*) You mean...Madame Arcati?

EDNA *appears in the doorway behind him. She carries a tray of coffee cups, etc.*

(indignantly) Well what are you looking at me for? *I* didn't do it.

ZOE *(rising suddenly)* He *did*. It's *him*. *(To the others) He* was the one in the clown suit. *(Her voice rising)* He was the one who *shot* her. *(To* VERNON*)* It *was* you, wasn't it? *You* stole that clown suit and killed a perfectly innocent woman. A woman who'd never harmed another living creature in her life. You *killed* her. *(She bursts into tears and flings herself into* LARRY's *arms)*

LARRY *and* ZOE *subside on to the chaise.*

ATHENE *(puzzled)* I thought we were talking about Octavia?

VERNON *(astounded)* She's off her rocker. I've been outside for the last half hour trying to find Mr Crayle.

AUGUSTUS *(snorting)* A likely story. Probably disposing of his body.

VERNON Body?

HENRIETTA Oh, yes. He's dead too. *(She rises)* And *you're* the one who did it.

EDNA *(suddenly)* No, he didn't. He *didn't*.

Everybody turns to look at her.

(moving into the room) It was *me*. *I* killed them.

HENRIETTA *(incredulously)* You? *(She sits again)*

VERNON *(anguished)* No.

EDNA *(fiercely)* I'm a good worker, I am, and they'd no right to say otherwise. Looking down their long noses and criticizing. So that's why I did it. That's why I killed them. And you can send for the police right now and I'll tell them exactly the same. *(She puts the tray down on the library table and glares at them defiantly)*

VERNON *(shaking his head)* I don't believe this. You've all gone stark staring bonkers. *(To the others)* She hasn't killed *anybody.* She couldn't have done. I've known her for ages.

EDNA *(insistently)* I did, Vernon. I *did.* I got dressed up as a clown and I shot 'em.

FABIA *(raising an eyebrow) Both* of 'em?

EDNA *(firmly)* Both of 'em.

> **FABIA** *begins to chuckle. After a moment,* **HENRIETTA,** **ATHENE** *and* **AUGUSTUS** *join in. As* **EDNA** *looks at them in bewilderment, the laughter grows louder.*

VERNON *(disgustedly)* Welcome to Loony Tunes. *(To the others)* She's lying, I tell you. She's lying.

FABIA *(spluttering)* Course she's lying. She no more killed 'em than *I* did. *(To* **EDNA***)* Crayle wasn't *shot,* darlin'. He got done in with a meat cleaver. Now why don't you toddle off back to the kitchen and leave us to discuss things in private, eh?

EDNA *(defensively)* Not if you're going to blame Vernon. He *couldn't* have killed anybody. He couldn't have.

ZOE *(glaring)* Well *somebody* did. And he's the most likely suspect.

LARRY *(cautiously)* We don't actually *know* that. I mean...if he *was* outside...

VERNON *(irritated)* Of course I was outside. I've even brought your things from the van. They're out in the hall. *(He indicates)*

LARRY In that case... *(He glances round them all),* it's got to be one of *us.*

> *The* **TOMBS** *exchange glances.*

AUGUSTUS *(snapping)* Rubbish. We wouldn't kill one of our own.

ATHENE *(qualifying the statement)* Unless the price was right.

FABIA And why kill Crayle? Without *him*, we'll have to wait years before getting our hands on the estate.

HENRIETTA Which also begs the question of who might like to see us *not* getting at it? *(She looks pointedly at* ZOE*)*

ZOE *(bridling)* As far as *I'm* aware, Miss Tomb, there's no-one else involved. The entire estate would be divided equally between the five surviving relations.

ATHENE *(correcting her)* Six.

The TOMBS *freeze.*

ZOE *(startled)* I beg your pardon? *(She stares at* ATHENE*)*

AUGUSTUS *(glaring at* ATHENE*)* Athene is mistaken. There were only five of us.

ATHENE *(defiantly)* No, Augustus. There *weren't.* *(Primly)* We mustn't cheat Vesta out of *her* share.

ZOE *(baffled)* Vesta?

ATHENE *(firmly)* Our aunt in Gravesend. She's ninety-seven and no-one ever mentions her because she once—

HENRIETTA ⎫
FABIA   ⎬ *(together)* Athene.
AUGUSTUS ⎭

ATHENE *(protesting)* But she *did.*

AUGUSTUS *(icily)* We are perfectly aware of what she did, Athene, which is precisely the reason we no longer acknowledge her existence.

ZOE *(stunned)* You mean...there's another one? *(Dazedly)* Oh, my God.

HENRIETTA *(frowning)* Something wrong?

ZOE *(snapping)* Of course there's something wrong. *(She remembers herself)* I mean... We'd no idea. We thought you were the last. *(Her mind races)* I'm sorry. But this changes everything. *Everything.*

FABIA I don't see why it should. As far as *we're* concerned, she don't even exist.

ZOE But in the eyes of the law, she *does*, and she's entitled to the same treatment as yourselves. We'll need her address... phone number...

HENRIETTA *(heavily)* Over my dead body. What she never gets to know about, she isn't going to grieve over. *(She sits again)*

ATHENE *(uneasily)* But she *does* know, Henrietta.

HENRIETTA *(snarling)* How can she know? None of us have... *(She stops as realization dawns)* You haven't? *(Incredulously)* You *didn't?*

The **TOMBS** *glare at* **ATHENE** *in disbelief.*

ATHENE *(blenching)* Only in passing. I mean... I wanted to know if Mr Crayle had sent *her* a letter, too. But he hadn't. She said...

AUGUSTUS *(in disbelief)* I cannot believe this, Athene. *(He raises his voice)* I cannot believe it. *(He thunders)* You have the audacity...the unbelievable *audacity*...to communicate with that—that raddled old *monster,* despite my explicit instructions to the contrary? *(He glares at her in fury)*

ATHENE *(clasping her ears)* I'm sorry, Augustus. I'm sorry.

AUGUSTUS *(savagely)* If our parents were alive today, they'd be turning in their graves. I shall never forgive you for this, Athene. Never.

FABIA *(heavily)* Well, now. Seems like we've got ourselves an entirely different ball game to what we *thought* we had. If Vesta's in on this, we could *all* be in trouble.

ZOE How do you mean?

FABIA From what *I* remember of her, she won't have taken kindly to being left out. And when something upsets her she does have a tendency to play nasty. Remember that Jehovah's Witness who kept pestering her?

The other TOMBS *react and* AUGUSTUS *quickly picks up his whisky and gulps it down.*

Took 'em six months to work out which bits were him and which were his *Watchtower.*

ATHENE *(hastily)* But she didn't *seem* annoyed, Fabia. Really, she didn't. She just said she might send someone down to keep an eye on things,

FABIA *(to the others)* Then that's it. And if she *did* do, it explains why Crayle and Octavia were murdered. *Him* to stop us getting our hands on the Estate, and *her* to teach the rest of us a lesson.

LARRY *(incredulously)* I don't believe this. You're telling us a ninety-seven year old *woman's* responsible for these murders?

HENRIETTA *(growling)* You'd better believe it.

VERNON *(in mock sympathy)* Ooh, she must be *such* a trial to you. *(He is annoyed)* Now just one minute. I might not be Miss Marple but I've been a policeman in six plays with the amateurs, and there's one thing I *have* learned about murder. The quicker you bring on your detective, the better. *I* say we get the police here right now and let *them* work it out.

LARRY *(nodding)* Exactly what I've been saying.

VERNON *(satisfied)* Right. I'll be back as soon as possible. *(In his best "butch" voice)* Nobody leave the house. *(He turns to exit)*

HENRIETTA *(rising)* Not so fast, nancy boy. How do we know *you're* not responsible? Let *you* out of here and we might never see you again.

FABIA She's right. *(She points the gun at* VERNON*)* You're staying just where you are, dearie.

VERNON *(stymied)* Well *somebody's* got to go. *(He looks at* LARRY *for support)*

LARRY *(uncomfortably)* I suppose *I* could try...but I might end up losing myself. I mean... I don't know the area, and that fog looks thicker than ever.

EDNA *(suddenly)* I could go.

VERNON *(defensively)* Oh, no, you couldn't. Not in that lot.

EDNA But it's only a few miles, and I know the way better than anybody. I *live* in Haslow, remember.

HENRIETTA *scowls.*

LARRY She's right. And she's the only one of us who couldn't possibly have killed them.

VERNON *(tartly)* And what if it *wasn't* one of us? What if it's this ninety-seven year old woman they've been going on about. She could be out there with a machine gun strapped to her zimmer frame, just waiting to blow the head off the first one to step outside. *(He gathers his courage)* No. A man's gotta do what a man's gotta do. *I'll* go for the police, and that's final. *(He glares at them all)*

FABIA *(unexpectedly)* All right, then, darlin'. *(She lowers the gun)* Off you go. And we'll see you when we see you.

ATHENE *(surprised)* But...

FABIA Like the man says...*somebody* has to go, and I don't fancy a five mile hike myself. Do you?

VERNON Right. Well that's settled, then. I'll see you all later. *(He turns to exit)*

EDNA *(anxiously)* Be careful Vernon.

VERNON Don't worry, darlin'. If anybody comes after me, I'll scream so loud I'll shatter their ear-drums.

VERNON *exits, bravely whistling or singing a military air, and the sound decreases to silence as he moves down the corridor.*

EDNA *(suddenly)* Would anybody like some coffee?

No-one replies.

(awkwardly) Well... I'll just leave it there, then. You can help yourselves.

EDNA *exits.*

There is another short silence.

ZOE *(to LARRY)* I'm not feeling well. I think I need to lie down.

LARRY *(concerned)* I'll help you upstairs.

They rise.

ZOE *(faintly)* It must be the shock. Seeing that poor woman killed.

LARRY Try to put it out of your mind. A rest'll do you the world of good. *(He assists her towards the door)*

ZOE *(gushing)* I'm so glad you're here, Mr Lewiss.

LARRY Larry. You can call me Larry.

LARRY *and* **ZOE** *exit into the hall.*

HENRIETTA *(balefully)* Excuse me while I'm sick. *(She pretends to retch)*

AUGUSTUS *(angrily to* **FABIA***)* Are you out of your mind, Fabia? Letting that *moron* go for the police? The last thing we want is *them* poking their noses into things that don't concern them.

ATHENE *(anxiously)* You never know *what* they'll find.

FABIA *(coldly)* They won't find anything...because he's not going to get there. *(She hands the gun to* **AUGUSTUS***)* Follow him down the drive and deal with him.

AUGUSTUS *(distastefully)* With a gun?

FABIA *(tartly)* There's no time for niceties. We've got to stop him. Just *do* it.

With a look of annoyance on his face, AUGUSTUS *moves to the bookcase and presses a concealed catch. The case pivots and he steps through to vanish.*

The bookcase closes behind him.

HENRIETTA *(picking up another sandwich)* And what about the rest of 'em? When do we deal with *them*? *(She takes a bite)*

FABIA Soon as I work out why our not-so-clever Mrs Mapleton finished off Crayle and Octavia. *(She sits on the chaise)*

ATHENE *(startled)* But the man in the clown suit...

FABIA Doesn't exist, darlin'. *She* killed Octavia. I knew it the minute I found 'em here. *(She explains)* When Tavie was shot, she was holding one of her "pins" ...I found it in her hand...and our innocent lookin' Mrs Mapleton had a teensy weensy spot of blood right here. *(She indicates on her own throat)* Now the way *I* see it...when she came back down here—

HENRIETTA *(interrupting)* Octavia tried to find out what was going on and the Mapleton woman shot her.

FABIA *(glaring at her, then nodding)* And if I hadn't walked in on them just as it happened, she'd have joined Crayle in the marsh with none of us being any the wiser.

ATHENE *(puzzled)* But why did she say *Augustus* did it? And then Mr Prewitt?

HENRIETTA *(pityingly)* To throw us off the scent, dim-wits. She knew the clown suit was missing and she knew about the passageways. If she made us think somebody else did it, she fancied she'd be in the clear.

FABIA Which is *exactly* why I let her think she'd got away with it. All we need to know now, is the *real* reason we were dragged down here. And once we do... *(She smiles in a cruel manner)*

ATHENE *(brightening)* Then...it's nothing to do with Aunt Vesta?

HENRIETTA *(glowering)* No thanks to you. *(Thoughtfully)* Though it certainly shook Madam Mapleton when she heard about her, didn't it? I wonder why that was? *(She takes another bite)*

FABIA *(slowly)* Perhaps... *(She stops)*

HENRIETTA *(stopping chewing)* What?

FABIA *(thoughtfully)* I wonder what'd happen to this place if we all dropped dead? Tonight, for instance. Who'd it *go* to?

HENRIETTA *(uninterestedly)* Who cares? We wouldn't be around to worry about it. *(She takes another bite and reaches for her milk glass)*

ATHENE *(uncertainly)* I suppose Aunt Vesta...

HENRIETTA *glowers at her.*

FABIA Yes, but if *she* didn't exist...or at least...nobody *knew* she existed...who'd it go to *then*?

HENRIETTA *(after a moment)* Government, I expect. *(She drinks her milk)*

FABIA *(pointedly)* Or to someone producing *another* will leaving everything to *them*.

ATHENE *(puzzled)* But they couldn't do. I mean...there isn't one, is there?

FABIA *(easily)* Never heard of *forgery*, darlin'?

HENRIETTA *(catching on)* And who better to forge a will than a crooked solicitor and his fancy-piece secretary? *(She frowns)* But what's the point? We're *not* dead.

FABIA *(pointedly)* Octavia is.

ATHENE *(incredulously)* You mean they wanted to kill *us*? But that's *criminal*.

HENRIETTA *(ignoring her)* So why'd she kill *him*?

FABIA Thieves fallin' out. Get rid of Crayle, and she collects the lot.

ATHENE *(indignantly)* Over my dead body.

FABIA Precisely. But what she *isn't* expecting, is for us to have worked it out. *(Scornfully)* Stupid cow. We've forgotten more about murder than she's ever dreamt of. *(She smiles)* Well... if it's games she wants to play, then I'm quite sure we can accommodate her. Don't you agree?

HENRIETTA *(grimly)* Let me deal with her. *(She puts down her glass)*

FABIA *(soothingly)* No, no, Hettie. Not yet. First we get rid of the others...*then* we have our fun.

There is the sound of a shot, off. They all turn their heads to look at the window.

(beaming) And there goes number one.

HENRIETTA And not before time. If there's one thing I can't stand, it's a pervert.

ATHENE *(eagerly)* So who do we do next?

FABIA *(glancing off into the hall)* You don't do anything, darlin'. The next one's all *mine*. *(She plumps her hair)*

LARRY *limps hurriedly into the room.*

LARRY *(breathlessly)* What was that? It sounded like a gunshot.

FABIA *(raising her eyebrows)* Gunshot?

LARRY Yes. It came from outside. *(He crosses to the window and peers out)*

FABIA Well I can't say *we* heard anything, *(to the others)* did we, girls?

HENRIETTA *and* **ATHENE** *shake their heads.*

LARRY *(puzzled)* But *I* heard it. As clear as anything.

ATHENE *(reasonably)* Perhaps a poacher, Mr Lewiss? Or someone shooting *vermin.*

LARRY *(incredulous)* In *this* fog? *(Anxiously)* Look. *Vernon's* out there. They could be shooting at him. *(He peers out of the window again)*

FABIA *(frowning)* Well, like I said, we didn't hear anything. But if Aunt Vesta *is* out there... *(To* HENRIETTA *and* ATHENE*)* Perhaps you'd better find Augustus. Ask him to check outside. Just to be on the safe side. *(She indicates with her head for them to go)*

ATHENE *(surprised)* But he's already...

HENRIETTA *(cutting her off)* Right. *(She grasps* ATHENE*'s hand)* Come on, sister, dear. We've got things to do.

She marches the bewildered ATHENE *out into the hall, closing the door.*

FABIA *(warmly)* Now why don't you rest that poorly leg of yours and sit next to me? *(She pats the chaise)* I want to hear all about your life in show business. And don't forget the naughty bits. *(She laughs)*

LARRY *(turning to look at her)* It doesn't seem to worry you at all, does it? I mean...a double murderer running around loose, and you haven't turned a hair.

FABIA It's all on the inside, darlin'. To tell you the truth, I'm scared to death. *(Her voice cracking)* I try to put a brave face on things, but underneath it all I'm shakin' like a leaf. It's not easy knowing you've got an homicidal maniac for an aunt. *(She sobs)* Nobody knows how I've suffered. *(She fumbles without success for a handkerchief)*

LARRY *(concerned)* I'm sorry. I didn't mean... *(He crosses to her and sits beside her)* Here... *(He fumbles in his pocket for his own handkerchief)* Use mine.

Before he can withdraw his hand, **FABIA** *turns to him and wraps herself around him forcing him backwards on to the head of the chaise.*

FABIA *(kissing him fiercely)* Oh, Mr Lewiss. Larry. You're so good to me.

LARRY *(struggling to free himself)* Fabia. No. Wait.

FABIA *(panting)* You're so strong. *(She kisses him)* So *virile.* So sexy.

LARRY *(flailing beneath her)* Please...

FABIA *(pulling out his shirt and struggling to tear it off him)* You'll protect me. I know you will. *(She kisses him, passionately)* You'll keep me safe. Oh, you darlin'. Oh, you sweetheart.

LARRY *(still flailing helplessly)* Help.

FABIA *(panting)* We don't need help, darlin'. I can manage this myself. *(She struggles to shed her jacket whilst still restraining him)*

Suddenly the french windows open and **VERNON** *staggers into the room. Blood is smeared on his cheek and streams down his neck from a wounded ear.*

VERNON *(gasping)* He's out there. In the garden. He tried to kill me. Ohhhh. *(His knees give way and he collapses backwards on to the floor)*

FABIA *freezes and gapes at him.*

LARRY *(struggling free of her)* Vernon. *(He rolls off the chaise and scrabbles to* **VERNON**'s *body, cradling his head)* Vernon.

VERNON *(moaning)* Don't let him kill me. Not just as I've got my Equity card.

LARRY *(anxiously)* Who was it, Vernon? Who *was* it?

FABIA *snatches up the poker and raises it to strike the back of* LARRY's *head.*

VERNON *(groaning)* Him. The Clown.

FABIA *looks stunned and lowers the poker.*

(weakly) He was waiting for me down the drive. If I hadn't put me foot in a pot-hole, he'd have shot me straight through the head. *(He groans)*

LARRY *looks at him in disbelief.*

FABIA So what did you do?

VERNON *(raising himself)* I picked myself up and asked him if he'd like to have another go. *(He is livid)* What do you *think* I did, you dozy mare? I ran for it. *(He groans)* Ohhhhh, I'm dying. I can feel my life-blood slipping away. *(Weakly)* Kiss me, Hardy. *(He slumps unconscious)*

FABIA *replaces the poker.*

LARRY *(anxiously)* Vernon. Vernon. *(He looks up)* He's fainted. *(He glances round)* Quick. We need something to stop the bleeding.

FABIA Try a tourniquet.

LARRY *(startled)* It's a *head* wound.

FABIA *(muttering)* Well, put it round his neck, then.

LARRY *(remembering)* Wait. Augustus. *He's* a doctor. Where is he?

FABIA *(hedging)* Haven't a clue, darlin'. Probably up in his room.

LARRY Get him down here. Quickly. No. I'll do it myself. You keep an eye on Vernon. *(He lowers* VERNON *gently to the floor and rises)* Try and make him comfortable.

LARRY *hurries out, leaving the doors open.*

FABIA *(watching him go)* Comfortable? *(She laughs quietly)* You'll be the death of me, darlin'. *(She looks down at VERNON)* So... You managed to dodge old Gussie, did you? Well, if that don't deserve a medal, I can't think what does. He may be a few pence short of a pound, but he could outshoot Annie Oakley standing on his head with both eyes shut. *(Thoughtfully)* Still...we have to stop this bleeding, haven't we? *(She picks up a cushion)* Perhaps a little *pressure* might help? *(She moves to his head, and sinks to her knees)* Only trouble with this method, darlin' ...the side effects are a bit unfortunate. They stop you *breathin'* as well. But then again...I'm sure you're not the complainin' type. *(She begins to lower the cushion on to his face)*

EDNA *(offstage; anxiously)* Vernon. *Vernon.*

FABIA *looks up furiously and quickly removes the cushion from his face to slide it under his head.*

EDNA *rushes into the room, sees him, and gives a gasp of horror.*

Vernon. *(She flings herself down beside him)* Wake up, Vernon. Say something. *(To FABIA)* He's not dead, is he? He's still breathing?

FABIA *(gritting her teeth)* 'Course he is. Passed out with shock, I expect. He'll be right as rain in no time.

EDNA *(looking at VERNON)* But all this *blood*?

FABIA *(forcing a smile)* Just a flesh wound, darlin'. Bit of sticking plaster'll soon fix that. Now why don't you get a towel and some water and we'll see if we can clean him up? Eh?

EDNA *(doubtfully)* And you're sure he'll be all right? *(She rises)*

FABIA Don't worry, darlin'. *I'll* see he's taken care of.

EDNA *moves reluctantly towards the door.*

And I should take them coffee things, if I were you. Don't look like nobody wanted any, after all.

EDNA *takes the tray of coffee things and exits.*

As soon as she is gone, FABIA *rips the cushion from beneath* VERNON*'s head.*

(grimly) Right. And this time there'll be *no* interruptions. *(She is about to place the cushion over his face again)*

The secret panel opens and the Clown, dressed as before, steps into the room. He carries a flower misting spray in one hand and a colourful bunch of artificial flowers in the other.

FABIA *sees him and her face blackens in fury as she rises.*

Are you out of your mind? You were supposed to kill him, not ponce about like a flamin' jack-in-a-box. *(Scornfully)* Augustus the crack-shot. More the flamin' crack-pot if you ask me. I should have known better than to trust *you* to do a job right. Now get rid of those flowers, take that stupid mask off and give me a hand to finish him.

The Clown does not move, but VERNON *begins to stir.*

(raising her voice) Did you hear me? *(She crosses towards him and tears the flowers out of his hand)*

He squirts a shot of spray into her face and she lets out a cry of shock and pain, dropping the flowers and claws at her eyes.

My eyes. I can't see. *(She flails helplessly)* Augustus. *(She suddenly stiffens in shock and shrieks)* Cyanide. *(Incredulously)* You've sprayed me with cyani... *(Her voice fades away and she clutches helplessly at her throat before collapsing to the ground)*

The Clown sprays another blast at her face.

VERNON *(dazedly raising himself)* I'm ready for my close-up, Mr de Mille. *(He sees* FABIA *and the Clown)* Ahhhhhhh.

The Clown bows deeply, waggles his fingers, turns and exits quickly through the passageway.

The panel closes. FABIA *twitches feebly and lies still.* VERNON *staggers groggily to his feet.*

(croaking) Help. *(He totters towards the door)* Help. *(Louder)* Help.

HENRIETTA *appears in the doorway.*

(gasping) The Clown. He's killed Fabia. He's behind the bookcase.

HENRIETTA *moves swiftly to the bookcase.*

EDNA *appears in the doorway and* VERNON *slumps into her arms.*

HENRIETTA *releases the secret catch and the bookcase opens.*

AUGUSTUS *stands in the opening, his face painted white and made up as a clown.*

HENRIETTA *(taken aback)* Augustus?

AUGUSTUS *topples to the ground, a huge kitchen knife embedded in his back. As* HENRIETTA *reacts,* VERNON *and* EDNA *scream in horror.*

The curtain falls.

Scene Two

The same. An hour later.

The bodies of **FABIA** *and* **AUGUSTUS** *have been removed and so have the flowers. The french windows are closed again, as is the secret panel, but otherwise the room is as before.*

ATHENE *sits in the wing chair, calmly sipping at a glass of sherry.* **HENRIETTA** *stands by the fireplace, gazing into the flames, a brooding expression on her face.* **ZOE** *sits on the chaise, clearly very tense, and* **LARRY** *stands by the library table.*

LARRY *(tightly)* I don't believe this. I just don't believe it. Not only do you move a body and mess up the evidence *once*, you go and do it a *second* time. What's wrong with you people? Don't you *want* this maniac caught?

ZOE Larry...

LARRY *(ignoring her)* You know what's going to happen, don't you? When we finally *do* get the police here, they're going to bang us *all* up for perverting the cause of justice. *(He moans)* It'll make every newspaper in the country... *(Horrified)* not to mention *television. (The realization hits him)* I'll never work again. What mother in her right mind's going to leave their kid alone with a murderer's accomplice? *(He sinks into the chair, a picture of misery)*

ATHENE *(unconcerned)* You really *should* try a glass of sherry, Mr Lewiss. It's very good for the nerves. *(She sips daintily)*

ZOE *(gritting her teeth)* Excuse me. *(She rises and moves towards the door)*

HENRIETTA *(looking up)* And where do you think you're going?

ZOE Not that it's any of your business, but I'm going to my room.

HENRIETTA Alone?

ZOE I don't see why not. We've already searched the house from top to bottom and found nothing. Whoever did these murders is long gone, and to be perfectly frank, this constant bickering is getting on my nerves. I need a cigarette.

ATHENE *(slightly shocked)* But they're very bad for your health, dear. Father wouldn't allow *anyone* to smoke in *his* house. No matter *who* they were.

VERNON enters, a large wad of padding strapped to his ear, and a pained expression on his face.

Though we always suspected *Augustus* had the occasional puff in his surgery.

VERNON *(acidly)* Well even *we* get sick at times.

LARRY *(jumping up)* How are you feeling?

VERNON *(peevishly)* How do you think I'm feeling? I've had half my ear shot off, lost five litres of blood and I've got a splitting headache. *(He grimaces)* I shall have nightmares for the rest of my life after this lot. *(He touches his ear padding, winces and speaks anxiously)* You don't think it'll spoil my looks, do you?

ZOE *(irritated)* Oh, stop whingeing. It's only a scratch.

VERNON *(indignantly)* It might only be a scratch to *you*, sweetie-pie, but it'll look like the flamin' Grand Canyon in Cinemascope.

ZOE gives him a withering glance and exits.

(bitterly) And to think that only an hour ago I could have been the new Donald O' Connor. Now I'll look like Claude Raines in *The Phantom of the Opera*.

LARRY *(blankly)* Who?

VERNON *(tiredly)* Never mind, dear. They were before your time. *(He closes his eyes and raises a hand to his temple)*

LARRY Would you like some paracetamol? There's probably a pack in my jacket. *(Ruefully)* I usually need them after a performance.

VERNON Right at this minute, I could cheerfully take cyanide.

ATHENE *(matter-of-factly)* Second shelf down on the left in the sick room. Next to the Antimony. *(She sips at her sherry)*

They look askance at her.

LARRY *(to VERNON)* I'll be back in a minute.

LARRY *exits.*

HENRIETTA *(calling)* And while you're at it, tell her to get a move on with that coffee. *(Grimly)* I want everybody here in the next five minutes. *(She moves down towards VERNON)* So. You've decided to join the living, have you?

VERNON *(defensively)* It wasn't my fault I had to lie down. It's a nasty thing is shock. I'm still all of a doo-dah. *(He sits at the table)*

HENRIETTA Then what are you doing out of bed?

VERNON *(uneasily)* There's something creepy about that room. It's like the Black Hole of Calcutta, even with all the lights on. And as for that four poster... *(He shudders)* Every time I looked up, I thought the top was coming down to suffocate me.

ATHENE *(scornfully)* How ridiculous. It wouldn't do anything of the kind. *(As an afterthought)* Not unless you switched the bedside lights off.

VERNON *gapes at her in disbelief.*

A fearful-looking EDNA *enters, carrying a tray of coffee things and a small plate of biscuits.*

HENRIETTA *(growling)* And about time.

EDNA *(sniffling)* I'm sorry, miss, but it's awful being in that kitchen on my own. I've never seen dead bodies before and I was shaking so much, I thought I was going to be sick. I had to leave everything and go to the toilet.

HENRIETTA *(tartly)* Then let's hope it's still hot. If there's one thing I can't stand, it's lukewarm coffee.

EDNA *deposits the tray on the library table.*

VERNON *(standing)* Well, pardon me for saying so, but a bit of sympathy mightn't come amiss. *(To EDNA; kindly)* I know just how you feel, darlin'. I'm still having palpitations myself.

EDNA *(face crumpling)* Oh, Vernon. I want to go home. *(She sobs)*

VERNON *(holding her)* Course you do, darlin'. And as soon as this fog's cleared, that's exactly where you're going. Now just you sit down till you're feeling better. *(He eases her into the chair)* You can have a nice drink of coffee and one of these biscuits.

EDNA *continues to sob.*

HENRIETTA *(tartly)* You're very free with other people's property, aren't you? If we wanted to drink coffee with the servants, we'd have it served in the kitchen. *(She moves to the table, picks up the coffee jug, then grimaces, puts it down again and looks at her hand. To EDNA, sharply)* You've slopped coffee down this handle. Go get a cloth and be quick about it. *(She wipes her palm on her skirt)*

VERNON *(firmly)* You stay where you are, dear. *I'll* do it. *(He moves towards the door)*

ATHENE *suddenly sniffs the air and frowns.*

HENRIETTA *(glowering at her)* And what's wrong with you?

ATHENE *(puzzled)* I can smell fish.

VERNON *and* HENRIETTA *sniff the air.*

HENRIETTA *(sourly)* I can't.

VERNON Me neither.

ATHENE Oh, it's only faint but I can smell it quite clearly. *(Proudly)* I've always had a keen nose.

HENRIETTA *(sourly)* You've always had a *long* nose. Comes from constantly sticking it in other folk's business. *(To* VERNON, *sharply)* Are you getting that cloth or aren't you?

VERNON *pulls a face and exits.*

(to EDNA*; grimly)* And as for you, madam, you can stop *that* noise before I stop it for you. If there's one thing I can't stand, it's snivelling females. *(She glares at her)*

EDNA *stops sobbing, sniffles and brushes her eyes.*

ATHENE *(pensively)* I'm sure I've smelled it before, you know. A long time ago. *(She frowns)* If only I could remember... *(She sinks into thought)*

LARRY *enters with the packet of tablets.*

LARRY *(displaying the packet)* Found them. *(He takes in the scene)* Something wrong?

HENRIETTA *(grimly)* Nothing that can't be cured by a quiet little chat. And that's just what we're going to have when the others get back. *(She indicates the chaise with a toss of her head)* Sit.

LARRY *hesitates, then moves to the chaise and sits.*

(with satisfaction) I've been doing some thinking, you see, and it seems to me that what's been going on here can be worked out quite easily. Wouldn't you agree, Mr Lewiss?

LARRY *(taken aback)* I... I don't know. I mean... Yes. If you say so.

HENRIETTA *(smiling nastily)* Oh, I *do* say so, Mr Lewiss. Most certainly I do.

VERNON *enters, carrying a dishcloth. He goes to the table, wipes the coffee pot handle and drops the cloth disdainfully on to the tabletop.*

And *another* thing I say is, it's time to put a stop to it. *(With menace)* Which is exactly what I'm going to do in the next few minutes.

VERNON *(sweetly)* Excuse the interruption, but shall I be Mother? *(He picks up the coffee pot)*

HENRIETTA *(ungraciously)* You can be Father Christmas, for all I care. Just get it poured before it's so cold we have to chip it out with an ice-pick. Milk and two sugars for me.

VERNON *begins to pour coffee.*

LARRY Same here, thanks. *(He remembers)* Oh, and I've got the tablets. *(He shows the box)*

VERNON Thanks, doll. You're a life saver.

HENRIETTA *(glancing at the doorway)* What's taking *her* so long? She's had time to *grow* the flaming tobacco.

LARRY Would you like me to look for her? *(He begins to rise)*

HENRIETTA *(sharply)* No. You can stay where you are. Nobody leaves the room till I've said what I have to say. *(With great emphasis)* Nobody.

LARRY *settles back again.* VERNON *hands her a cup of coffee which she sips at tentatively.*

ATHENE *(suddenly)* Great Uncle Claudius.

VERNON *hands a cup of coffee to* EDNA.

HENRIETTA *(squinting at her)* What?

ATHENE *(beaming)* It was Great Uncle *Claudius*.

VERNON *crosses to* LARRY *with a cup.*

HENRIETTA *(irritated)* Wha waz?

ATHENE *(brightly)* That's where I smelled it before.

HENRIETTA *(slurring her words)* Whazz are you blabbling aboull? Zmelt whazz? *(She blinks as if to clear her vision and sways as if disorientated)*

EDNA, LARRY *and* VERNON *look at her curiously.*

ATHENE The fishy smell, of course.

HENRIETTA *unsteadily puts down her cup.*

HENRIETTA Whazz haraming? Iz all shpinning.

LARRY *(putting his cup down and half rising)* Are you all right?

HENRIETTA *(bewildered)* Veel ztrange. Can't shee propery. *(She puts her hand to her head)* Eysh hurt. *(She sags against the table)*

EDNA *quickly rises to assist her.*

ATHENE *(putting her glass down and rising)* You see? It's *exactly* like Great Uncle Claudius.

HENRIETTA *(mumbling)* Ditty. *(She clutches at her throat)* Carn breath.

ATHENE *(recalling)* Dizziness. Incoherence. Loss of vision. Difficulty in breathing...

VERNON *(hastily)* Sit her down here. *(He indicates the chaise)*

HENRIETTA *(faintly)* Hel me. *(She falls to the floor, convulsing weakly)*

LARRY *and* VERNON *hurry to her.*

ATHENE *(triumphantly)* Followed by collapse and convulsions.

EDNA *(horrified)* What's wrong with her? What is it?

ATHENE *(matter-of-factly)* She's been poisoned. *(She smirks)* With nicotine.

LARRY *(looking up)* Nicotine?

ATHENE *(beaming)* There's no doubt about it. It used to be *very* popular in the old days. Absorbed by the skin, you see. You could smear it on a door knob and whoever touched it would be dead in minutes. *(She titters delightedly)* That's what must have been on the coffee-pot handle.

HENRIETTA *lies still.*

LARRY *(aghast)* We've got to get a doctor.

ATHENE Oh, it's much too late for that, dear. She'll be quite dead by this time. *(She sits again and reclaims her glass)*

EDNA *gives a strangled cry.* LARRY *quickly feels for* HENRIETTA*'s pulse.*

LARRY *(horrified)* She's right. *(He stands and rubs his hand on his trousers)*

VERNON *(staring at the body in fascination)* Oh, no. We haven't to carry *her* down to the vaults as well, have we? I nearly ruptured myself with the last one.

LARRY *(firmly)* We don't touch anything. Anything at all. She stays right where she is till the police have seen her. We've destroyed enough evidence already.

EDNA *(distressed)* But we can't just leave her there.

ZOE *enters.*

ZOE *(seeing* HENRIETTA*)* Oh, my God. What happened?

ATHENE *(scornfully)* As if you didn't know.

VERNON She's been poisoned. With nicotine.

ZOE *(bewildered)* But why should *I* know anything about it?

ATHENE Because you're the one responsible. *(Peeved)* You ought to be ashamed of yourself. Murdering people in their own home. *(She puts her glass down)* It wouldn't be too bad if you were one of the family, but you haven't even got *that* excuse. *(She rises)* If you'll forgive my saying so, Mrs Mapleton, you're nothing but a common outsider. And what's even worse. A complete *amateur*.

ATHENE *exits in outraged dignity.*

There is a momentary silence.

ZOE *(shakily)* She's mad. I haven't killed anyone.

LARRY *(quietly)* Somebody has.

ZOE Why couldn't it have been you... *(She indicates* VERNON*)* or him... *(She indicates* EDNA*)* or her? She could even have killed them *herself.* She probably *did.* She's a mass murderer. They *all* were.

They stare at her.

LARRY *(slowly)* I think you'd better explain.

ZOE *(taking a deep breath)* You're right. But... *(She glances at* HENRIETTA*'s body)* Could someone get rid of that? Take her next door or something.

LARRY *(shaking his head)* The police'll want to examine her where...

ZOE *(cutting in)* It won't make any difference. When you've heard what I have to say, you'll understand. *Please.*

LARRY *and* VERNON *exchange glances.*

LARRY *(finally)* Give me a hand?

LARRY *and* VERNON *distastefully pick up the body, grimacing under the strain.*

VERNON Oooof. Talk about dead weight.

LARRY *glowers at him.*

(wincing) Sorry. Slip of the tongue.

They stagger out into the hall with her.

EDNA *watches in fascination.* ZOE *moves to the window and looks blankly out.*

After a few moments, VERNON *and* LARRY *return.*

LARRY *(to* ZOE*)* Well?

ZOE *turns to face them.*

ZOE *(deliberately)* Our office in Burnham has handled the Tombs' business affairs for the last sixty years, or so. Perhaps you've heard of them? Penworthy, Venner and Crayle.

LARRY *(shaking his head)* I'm a Londoner myself.

EDNA *and* VERNON *look blank.*

ZOE Well anyway, one of the partners was actually here when whoever it was wiped everyone out...including him. Mortimer got the job of winding up the estate and found out something incredible. The Tomb family were mass murderers. For hundreds of years they'd been professional assassins and were so damned good at it, that no-one suspected a thing.

LARRY *(incredulously)* Come on.

ZOE *(flatly)* It was all in their records. Mozart. The "Marie Celeste". Tchaikovsky. Lord Lucan. Take your pick. I can give you hundreds more.

VERNON Lord Lucan? *(He is stricken)* Oh, and I used to love those Old Mother Riley films. *(He collapses into the chair)*

LARRY *(frowning)* Old Mother Riley? I thought that was *Arthur* Lucan.

VERNON Was it? *(He thinks)* Oh, yes. Sorry. *(He looks contrite)*

ZOE The trouble was, not all the Tombs were dead. There were various relatives all over the countryside and if he opened his mouth about what he'd discovered, he wouldn't have had a snowball in Hell's chance of surviving. His only hope was to lure them here, trap them, and hand them over to the police together with all the evidence.

EDNA But why didn't he call them to begin with?

ZOE *(drily)* Obviously you've no idea how incompetent the CPS are. Investigations could drag on for months. We'd both have been dead before the case came to court, and the evidence would have vanished without trace.

LARRY You said...both?

ZOE Mortimer and I had no secrets. I'd been with him for years. When this was over, we were going to be married. Oh, I know he was older, but what did age matter? He was a wonderful, generous, warm hearted man. *(She sits in the wing chair and fights to control her tears)*

LARRY *(uncomfortable)* He...er...he seemed a bit on the tetchy side to me.

ZOE *(incredulously)* Tetchy? He was worried about your *safety*. Here we were...in a house filled with mass murderers... and you come blundering into it. Is it any wonder he was tetchy? *(She dabs at her eyes)*

LARRY *(abashed)* I'm sorry. I didn't know.

VERNON *(indignantly)* And what about *us*? We could have got up in the morning and found out we'd been murdered during the night.

ZOE There was nothing for *you* to be worried about. He was going to put something in the drinks. To knock them out. Once they were unconscious, we'd tie them up and I'd go for the police. *(She sniffles)* But somehow they found out. *(She dabs her eyes)*

EDNA *(incredulously)* So they killed him?

ZOE *(nodding)* After he vanished, I was in a panic. I gave them the drinks but nothing happened. He couldn't have had time to do it. I was terrified they'd realize I was helping him and I'd be next on the list, but I didn't know what to do. And then Octavia was killed.

LARRY *(nodding)* By whoever stole my costume. *(He frowns)* But why kill *her*?

ZOE It was probably *my* fault. After Mortimer vanished, they cornered me in here and I had to tell them *something*. So I told them the estate would be shared by the surviving relations. I couldn't have said anything better. They all hated each other and Athene must have decided to eliminate the rest and collect the lot.

VERNON *(incredulous)* Athene? *(He looks out into the hall)*

ZOE *(nodding)* It has to be. She's the only one left.

EDNA But why try to kill Vernon?

VERNON *(indignantly)* Yes. What had *I* done?

ZOE Isn't it obvious? You were going for the police. She couldn't allow that to happen. It would have ruined everything.

LARRY But...that couldn't have been Athene. She was in here with Fabia and Henrietta. I saw her myself.

ZOE *(impatiently)* Then maybe it was Augustus.

EDNA But he was dead, miss...behind the bookcase.

VERNON *(tartly)* In that case, there's only one other person it *could* be. Old Granny Vesta with her double-barrelled zimmer frame.

LARRY *(thoughtfully)* Unless, of course...

VERNON What?

LARRY Well, this may sound a bit crazy, but...how do we know Crayle *is* dead? I mean...no-one's seen his body. Perhaps he's hiding in one of those secret passageways, just waiting for opportunities to bump them all off?

ZOE *(scathingly)* This isn't an Agatha Christie melodrama, Mr Lewiss. You're speaking about the man I loved, and that woman *killed* him. I owe it to his memory to see that she pays for it. *(She mops at her eyes)*

VERNON So...what are we going to do?

ZOE There's only one thing we *can* do. She's not going to let us leave here alive, is she? We've seen and heard too much. We've got to get her before she can get us.

EDNA *(aghast)* You mean...we've got to kill her?

LARRY *(quickly)* Now just a minute.

ZOE *(standing)* Of course not. We simply carry on with Mortimer's plan. Drug her and call the police. There's all kinds of pills and potions in the sick-room down the hall. Something's got to do the trick.

VERNON *(uncertainly)* Can't we just grab her? I mean...there's four of us and only one of her.

ZOE We can't take the chance. Who knows what she's got hidden on her? Remember those hair pins Octavia wore.

LARRY *(after a moment)* I'll see what's in the sick-room. *(He hesitates)* But how do we get her to take it? I mean...we can't *force* it down her.

ZOE *(glancing at the drinks table)* The sherry. She always drinks sherry. We'll put it in that.

LARRY *(doubtfully)* I hope you're right about this.

ZOE *(insistently)* I am. I know I am.

> **LARRY** *looks at her for a moment, then exits.*

VERNON What do you want us to do?

ZOE Anything that won't arouse suspicion. Just act normal.

VERNON *(drily)* If I acted *that*, dear, she'd have something to be suspicious about. *(Decisively)* I'll get some logs for the fire.

EDNA *(helpfully)* And I could make more sandwiches. There's still some tongue left.

VERNON *(aghast)* Tongue? *(He shudders)* Oh, I couldn't eat anything that came out of an animal's *mouth*. Haven't we any eggs?

EDNA *(forcing a smile)* I'll see what I can find.

VERNON *and* **EDNA** *exit.*

ZOE watches them go then takes a small bottle of liquid from her pocket and hurries to the drinks table. She opens the bottle and adds a few drops to all the decanters, then re-caps it, slips it back into her pocket and smiles in satisfaction.

ZOE And this time there'll be no mistake.

LARRY *enters holding a small bottle of colourless liquid.*

LARRY I found this.

She turns to face him.

(showing the bottle) Chloral hydrate. If I've got my chemistry right, it's what they used to call "knockout drops". Should put her to sleep for quite a few hours.

ZOE Perfect.

LARRY *(doubtfully)* The only thing is...I'm not sure of the dosage. Too much of it could kill her.

ZOE We'll have to take that risk. There's no other way. I promise you. *(She picks up the sherry decanter)* Here.

LARRY *(taking it)* I'll give it a couple of teaspoonsful. *(He takes the decanter to the library table, puts it down, removes the stopper, unscrews the top of the chloral hydrate and picks up a teaspoon. Uncertainly)* Here goes. *(He pours two teaspoonfuls into the sherry, re-stoppers the decanter, shakes it and holds it up to the light to peer at it)* All we have to do now is to get her to drink it.

ZOE *(confidently)* Leave that to me. And as soon as we've got her safely under lock and key, we can have a celebratory drink of our own. *(She takes the decanter from him and returns it to the drinks table)*

LARRY *(re-capping the bottle)* I'd better take this back. Just in case. *(He hesitates)* You're sure we're doing the right thing?

ZOE Trust me.

He turns to exit and meets ATHENE *as she enters carrying a gloomily jacketed novel in which a leather bookmark marks her place.*

Ignoring him, she crosses to the wing chair and settles herself.

LARRY *quickly exits.*

(making conversation) Night-time reading, Miss Tomb?

ATHENE *(primly)* I always read a little before retiring.

ZOE *(thinking quickly)* Would you like a glass of sherry? *(She picks us the decanter)*

ATHENE No, thank you. One per night is quite sufficient. *(She opens the book)*

ZOE *(pressing)* It might help you relax...especially after the terrible things that have happened.

ATHENE *(startled)* What terrible things?

The bookmark slides to the floor.

ZOE *(nonplussed)* The murders.

ATHENE *(relaxing)* Oh, those. *(She smiles)* Yes. I suppose they must seem terrible to you...being only an amateur. But I assure you, this house has seen far more terrible things than *you* could ever imagine. *(Dreamily)* There was the gentleman from the Inland Revenue, for instance... Wouldn't take no for an answer. *(Brightly)* I can never look at a casserole these days without thinking of him. *(She looks around)* Now where did I put my bookmark? *(She fusses)*

ZOE *(spotting it)* Allow me. *(She puts down the decanter; moves round and picks up the bookmark, offering it to* ATHENE*)*

ATHENE Thank you. *(She opens the cover)* Just pop it in there, will you?

> ZOE *does so and* ATHENE *closes the cover on it.*

Have you ever read an Ermyntrude Ash book, Mrs Mapleton? *(She displays the book)* Not as clever as Catrin Collier but nevertheless... *(She glances at the portrait above the fireplace)* She was Uncle Septimus's favourite author.

ZOE I don't get much time for reading, I'm afraid. Too busy with all the legal work.

ATHENE *(archly)* All work and no play make Jill a dull girl, Mrs Mapleton. *(She changes her tone)* But of course...you *do* play, don't you? *(Sharply)* Stupid little games that wouldn't fool a child.

ZOE *(shaken)* I'm sorry?

ATHENE *(sighing)* Poor Mrs Mapleton. You've really no idea who you're dealing with, have you? *(Sadly)* That's always the trouble with amateurs. They never plan properly. That's why they get found out.

ZOE *(tightly)* I don't know what you mean.

ATHENE *(gently)* Don't you? Oh, I think you *do*, dear. You were going to kill us all...you and Mr Crayle. Poison in the drinks, wasn't it? But what you *didn't* know was that *you* were going to die too. You see...you weren't his only partner. Someone else was playing games too. And you... *(She shrugs)* well... you were expendable.

ZOE *(forcing a scornful laugh)* This is ridiculous. What other partner?

ATHENE *(mildly)* Why, his lover, of course.

ZOE *(scornfully)* Lover? He was almost eighty.

ATHENE *Some* people are attracted to older men. *(She displays the book)* Just read Miss Ash. All her heroines marry older men.

ZOE You're not telling me... *(Incredulously)* You and *him*? *(Dismissively)* Don't make me laugh.

ATHENE Oh, no, dear. I'm afraid Mr Crayle would have had as much use for me as he had for you. His fancies lay in quite *another* direction.

ZOE I don't understand. *(She frowns)* You're not saying he was *gay*, are you?

ATHENE *regards her in silence.*

(incredulously) Crayle was gay?

ATHENE Such a dreadful misuse of a beautiful word. But yes. I'm afraid he was. And as soon as we'd all been disposed of, he and his boyfriend were going to live happily ever afterwards on *our* money. *(She puts the book down)*

ZOE *(realizing)* Prewitt. It was Prewitt, wasn't it? *(Bitterly)* I should have *known* he'd have something to do with it. Where is he? I'll *kill* him.

ATHENE *(mildly)* Too late, I'm afraid. I've already *dealt* with Mr Prewitt. He was gathering logs in the woodshed. *(She smiles nastily)* So dangerous, aren't they, axes? Even when they're rusty.

ZOE *(staring at her)* My God.

ATHENE And now—it's your turn. *(She rises and moves towards her)*

ZOE *(backing away)* Keep away from me. *(She calls loudly)* Larry. *(She screams)* Larry.

ATHENE *(halting by the library table)* Oh, it's no use calling for help. You're dead already, you see. Nicotine isn't the only poison that can be absorbed through the skin. There's

Endrin, for instance...or Ethylene... *(Pointedly)* or the one that was on the bookmark.

ZOE *gapes at her, then looks at her hand in disbelief.*

It should be taking effect any time now.

ZOE *(aghast)* You bitch. You devious old *bitch. (She scrubs furiously at her hand)* No. No. *(She screams)* Noooooooo.

ATHENE *turns away as* LARRY *comes hurrying in.*

LARRY *(startled)* What is it? What's happened?

ZOE *(hysterically)* She's poisoned me. She's poisoned me. She's killed Vernon and she's poisoned *me. (She lurches towards the desk, snatches up the paper knife and before anyone can react, rushes at* ATHENE *and stabs her)*

ATHENE*'s eyes open wide, then she shudders and falls to the ground.*

(dazedly) Help me, Larry. Help me. *(She drops the knife. She falls into* LARRY*'s arms, convulses and goes limp)*

He lowers her to the ground as EDNA *comes rushing in.*

EDNA *(worried)* What is it? Who screamed? *(She sees the bodies and screams)*

LARRY *(hastily)* Don't look. Don't look. *(He rises and puts his arms around her)*

EDNA *(sobbing)* I can't stand any more. I can't.

LARRY *(soothingly)* It's all right. It's all right. It's all over. *(He looks at the bodies)* It's all over.

EDNA *(pulling away from him)* Vernon? Where's Vernon? *(She looks around anxiously)*

LARRY *(gently)* I'm sorry.

EDNA *bursts out sobbing again and buries her face in* LARRY*'s chest.*

Come and sit down.

He leads her to the chaise and they sit.

It's all right. We're quite safe now.

EDNA *(sniffling)* How did it happen? *(She blinks away tears)*

LARRY *(looking at the bodies)* I'm not sure. But it looks like Zoe was right. Athene *was* the murderer. She killed Vernon and all the others...and somehow poisoned Zoe. But before it had time to take effect, Zoe grabbed the knife and stabbed her. *(He shakes his head in bewilderment)* I can't believe it. Three hours ago, there were ten of us...and now there's just you and me.

EDNA *begins sobbing again.*

(frowning) The only thing is... I still don't understand how she managed to shoot Vernon. She was here in the room when I heard the shot and came in. And he was quite positive it was the *clown* who fired at him. It doesn't make sense.

EDNA *(sniffling)* What's it matter now? They're all *dead.*

LARRY *(sighing)* Well... I suppose we'd better get our coats and walk into Haslow. We can get the police out here and the rest'll be up to them. *(He stands)* Are you feeling up to it?

EDNA *(sniffling and looking up)* There's just *one* thing...

LARRY Yes?

EDNA You *did* say you'd never been here before?

LARRY That's right.

EDNA *(sniffling)* But when I first let you in, you said you'd seen a signpost pointing to Haslow.

LARRY Just down the road. Yes.

EDNA *(frowning)* But how did you know that's how it's pronounced? All the signposts say Hag's Hollow.

LARRY *(amused)* Like I told you... I'm a children's entertainer. There were a couple of kids at the party who lived there. I remembered them telling me about it. Now come on. Get your coat and we'll make a start. *(He pauses)* Mind you, *(he looks out of the window)* it's still pretty grim out there. Perhaps we'd better have a warmer before we go.

EDNA *(puzzled)* Warmer?

LARRY A nice glass of sherry. *(He smiles)* It'll put some colour into your cheeks.

EDNA *(uncertainly)* I don't know. I've never had sherry before.

LARRY Then you're in for a surprise, I promise you. *(He crosses to the drinks table and picks up the sherry decanter)* One sip of this, and you'll think you're in heaven. *(He pours out a glass)* Who knows? Perhaps you *will* be. *(He hands it to her)*

EDNA *(embarrassed)* Thank you. *(She takes it)* Aren't you having one?

LARRY *(returning to the drinks table)* I think I'll stick to brandy. *(He picks up the brandy decanter and pours a drink)*

As he does so, the secret panel opens behind him, and the Clown steps silently into the room holding a large cardboard cup of cola with a thick straw in it. **LARRY** *picks up his glass, turns to* **EDNA** *and raises it in a toast.*

Bottoms Up. *(He sees the Clown and reacts)*

The Clown executes a deep bow, then straightening again, wags one finger at **LARRY** *in an admonitory fashion.*

(recovering himself) Who are you? And what are you doing with that costume?

EDNA *turns to see the Clown.*

(angrily) Say something, can't you?

The Clown raises his free hand and takes off the mask. It is **VERNON**.

(stunned) Vernon. *(He glances at* **ATHENE***)* She said you were dead.

VERNON smiles. *His whole demeanour has changed. The effeminate pose is dropped, though he remains sardonic and slightly flippant.*

VERNON As Oscar Wilde once said...or was it Mark Twain...? "The reports of my death have been greatly exaggerated". *(To* **EDNA***)* Hallo, sweetie. I shouldn't drink that if I were you. Larry's put something *rather* nasty in it and it wouldn't do a *thing* for your complexion. *(To* **LARRY***)* And as for *you...* I've a good mind to slap your legs. Here's me, flogging my guts out, and camping it up something rotten, and all the time we've got a *real* queen in our midst. Talk about *deceitful. (He drops the mask on to the table)* Oh. And you should have found a better place to hide *this* little number. *I* found it easily.

LARRY *(icily)* I don't know what you're talking about.

VERNON You mean you weren't Crayle's boyfriend? *(Scornfully)* Come on. I was in the passageway back there when he spoke to you on the phone...though I didn't realize it was you at the time. *(Admiringly)* You really fooled me, you know. I thought you were the real McCoy.

LARRY *(tightly)* Who are you?

VERNON Vernon Prewitt, of course. *(He indicates* **EDNA***)* And this is my lovely half-sister. *(Confidentially)* Vesta Tomb's our maternal grandmother.

LARRY *gapes at them in disbelief.*

When Athene spilled the beans about the rest of the family being invited down here, Vesta had a feeling that something wasn't right, so she sent *us* down to keep an eye on things. The employment agency's been one of her sidelines for years. It was the perfect cover.

EDNA *(in a quite different tone)* The only disadvantage was having to dress up in these things and pretend to be half witted. We're quite good at what we *do* do, actually.

LARRY So it was *you* who killed Mortimer?

VERNON And replaced the poisoned drinks. But we didn't know who his partner was. *I* thought it was one of the family...

EDNA And I thought it was Zoe. Neither of us suspected you.

LARRY *(to* VERNON*)* But one of them tried to kill you.

VERNON *(ruefully)* Yes. Though I hadn't gone down the drive as they expected. I'd gone upstairs to look for *your* missing clown costume. That's when I saw Augustus going out, and somebody else following him with a knife a few seconds later. I couldn't tell who it was because of the fog, and by the time I got downstairs, they'd gone. All I *did* find was a pool of blood and the gun. I knew I had to get back inside, so I ripped my ear with a bramble, fired the gun, then rushed back here to do my Camille bit. The thing was... I wasn't expecting you to kill again so quickly, and I'd tossed the gun into the pond. That's why I couldn't stop you killing Fabia.

LARRY So you don't have the gun now? *(He smiles)* What a shame. Because I've got its twin right here. *(He pulls his gun out of his jacket)*

VERNON *and* EDNA *react.*

VERNON Oops.

LARRY And now I'll finish what I started. Pour your brother a sherry, Edna, *(He points the gun at her)* I'm sure he's dying to try one.

VERNON I'd rather stick to this, if you don't mind. *(He holds up the coke cup)*

LARRY I'm sure you would...but I insist. *(He indicates to* EDNA *with the gun)*

VERNON That's funny. So do I. *(He puts the straw in his mouth, tugs it out of the cup, aims the straw at* LARRY *and blows hard)*

LARRY *jerks as though stung and slaps at his neck then turns to look at* VERNON.

LARRY What the hell was that?

VERNON *(apologetically)* Curare.

LARRY *points the gun at* VERNON *to shoot, then his arm wavers and his head sags to one side.*

Nighty night. *(He waggles his fingers)*

LARRY *slumps to the floor and lies still.*

EDNA *(standing)* That was close.

VERNON *(shrugging)* Not really. There's not much difference between a blow-pipe and one of these. And I've always been a crack shot with a peashooter. *(He glances at* ATHENE*)* Pity about Aunt Athene, though. I quite liked *her*.

EDNA Yes. She caught on fast when I told her who we *really* were. Still...it'll make Gran happy. Now the rest of them have gone, she's bound to inherit this place. And she's always loved it, hasn't she?

VERNON Yes, but I can't think why. Still... I can see her now. Queen of all she surveys. *(He frowns)* Mind you... I don't know what he'd have thought about it. *(He jerks his thumb at the portrait behind him)* They hadn't spoken for sixty years. But he'd be glad it was staying in the family. *(He turns to look at the portrait)* Wouldn't you, Uncle Septimus?

The portrait falls off the wall and crashes heavily to the ground. VERNON *and* EDNA *look at it, then look at each other.*

EDNA
VERNON } *(together; heavily)* Charming.

They burst into laughter and exit arm in arm as—.

—the curtain falls.

FURNITURE AND PROPERTY LIST

ACT I

Scene One

On stage: Immense black walnut fireplace with heavily carved wooden fender and huge firedogs of brass. *On it:* outsize vases
Poker
Portrait of Septimus Tomb in thick gold frame
Thick hearth rug
Massive empty bookcases, with dusty shelves and fine mesh doors
Thick velvet drapes hanging from a matching pelmet
Coffee-coloured net curtains
Key in french windows
Drinks table. *On it:* cut glass decanters containing brightly coloured liquids, collection of glasses and goblets
Comfortable leather wing chair on a swivel or easy glide castors
Massive Gothic doors of black walnut, each with large brass knob
Old-fashioned roll-top desk. *In it:* collection of quill pens, inkwell, papers, paper knife, quill pen, etc.
Wall-mounted outdated internal telephone
Table. *On it:* massive, leather tooled family Bible, in faded brown and gold
Leather-topped library table
Chair
Chaise-longue with cushions
Cobwebs

Off stage: Plastic cleaning box containing feather duster, cloths, spray polishes, brass cleaner, air freshener, and kitchen roll (**Vernon**)
Slim grey folder containing thin sheaf of typewritten papers (**Crayle**)

Scrap of paper (**Edna**)
Tray of duplicate decanters to the ones on table
(**Crayle**)
Large flashy handbag (**Fabia**)

Personal: **Vernon:** pink rubber cleaning gloves
Edna: handkerchief, thick round spectacles, watch
(worn throughout)
Zoe: notepad and pen
Crayle: matches, badly made hairpiece (worn
throughout)
Octavia: steel-rimmed spectacles, two large steel
pins (worn throughout)
Vernon: wide-brimmed hat, long mohair scarf,
shoulder bag
Augustus: monocle
Larry: garish hat with huge daisy trim, curly bright
coloured wig

Scene Two

On stage: As before

Off stage: Blood-stained meat cleaver (**Athene**)
Gun (**Clown**)

ACT II

Scene One

Set: Dinner plate, piled high with sandwiches
Glass of milk

Re-set: Paper knife on desk

Offstage: Tray of coffee cups, etc. (**Edna**)
Flower misting spray, colourful bunch of artificial
flowers (**Clown**)

Personal: **Larry:** handkerchief
Zoe: handkerchief

Scene Two

Strike: Flowers

Set: Teaspoon
             Clown's mask

Off stage: Tray of coffee things, small plate of biscuits (**Edna**)
            Packet of tablets (**Larry**)
            Dishcloth (**Vernon**)
            Small bottle of colourless liquid (**Larry**)
            Glossily jacketed novel with leather bookmark
              (**Athene**)
            Large cardboard cup of cola with thick straw
              (**Vernon**)

Personal: **Vernon:** large wad of padding strapped to his ear
            Zoe: small bottle of liquid
            Larry: gun

LIGHTING PLOT

Property fittings required: wall lights, chandelier
1 interior. The same throughout

ACT I, Scene One

To open: Darkness with faint haze from outside and fireglow

Cue 1   Doors open   (Page 2)
          Bring up light from hall

Cue 2   **Vernon** turns on lights   (Page 2)
          Bring up general lighting

Cue 3   **Edna** turns off lights   (Page 33)
          Fade out lighting except fireglow

ACT I, Scene Two

To open: Semi-darkness

Cue 4   Doors open   (Page 33)
          Bring up light from hall

Cue 5   **Zoe** turns on lights   (Page 34)
          Bring up general lighting

ACT II, Scene One

To open: Overall general lighting

No cues

ACT II, Scene Two

To open: Overall general lighting

No cues

EFFECTS PLOT

ACT I

Cue 1 **Crayle:** "Mr Prewitt..." (Page 11)
Hammering at main door off

Cue 2 **Octavia** smiles insanely (Page 17)
Hammering at main door off

Cue 3 **Edna:** "...get this clean before dinner." (Page 23)
Loud hammering at main door off

Cue 4 **Edna:** "Well..." (Page 26)
Hammering at main door off

Cue 5 **Crayle** closes passageway entrance (Page 32)
Internal phone buzzes

Cue 6 **Crayle** replaces receiver (Page 32)
Internal phone buzzes almost at once

Cue 7 **Clown** fires the gun (Page 56)
Backup gunshot (optional)

ACT II

Cue 8 **Fabia:** "...then we have our fun." (Page 71)
Sound of gunshot off

THIS
IS
NOT
THE
END

Lightning Source UK Ltd.
Milton Keynes UK
UKHW021254061022
410037UK00008B/28

Some months have passed since the ghastly events in Monument House, well known to those familiar with *A Tomb with a View*. Now Mortimer Crayle, the crusty old lawyer, and his secretary Zoe, have gathered the last remaining Tomb family members (as offbeat a bunch as the original occupants) at the old house, ostensibly to inform them about their inheritance. But Crayle has designs on the inheritance which demand the death of all Tombs. Fog descends on the gloomy mansion and in the cobwebby corridors things – and people – are seldom what they seem. With poison in every decanter and mysterious disappearances into secret passageways, host and guests alike join the increasing number of bodies in the cellar. A glorious spoof – a worthy sequel to *A Tomb with a View* – although previous acquaintance with the Tombs is not required.

| CASTING | 6 women, 4 men

SAMUEL FRENCH *Acting* Editions

✓ Clear text and large margins for practical use

✓ Choice of sizes and bindings to suit how you use playtexts

✓ Additional features help bring the play to life

samuelfrench.co.uk
samuelfrenchltd
samuel french uk

ISBN 978-0-573-01917-3
90000
9 780573 019173

PREPARE TO MEET THY TOMB

By
NORMAN ROBBINS

SAMUEL FRENCH